# DESIRE AND UNITY

Emmanuel–Marie Le Fébure du Bus

# DESIRE AND UNITY

## Augustinian Spirituality for Today

*Translated by Michael J. Miller*

IGNATIUS PRESS    SAN FRANCISCO

Original French edition:
*Désir et Unité*
© 2019 Éditions Tallandier, Paris

Cover art
*The Four Doctors of the Western Church*
*Saint Augustine of Hippo (354–430 A.D.)*
Attributed to Gerard Seghers (1591–1651)
Wikimedia Commons image in the Public Domain

Cover design by Roxanne Mei Lum

© 2022 by Ignatius Press, San Francisco
All rights reserved
ISBN 978-1-62164-444-6 (PB)
ISBN 978-1-64229-189-6 (eBook)
Library of Congress Control Number 2021952111
Printed in the United States of America ∞

*To Mary, whom Saint Augustine
calls the "Mother of unity"*

# CONTENTS

# INTRODUCTION

Like everyone else, he stood in line to greet the pope. The Jubilee of Artists, in the year 2000, made that encounter possible. Pope John Paul II pointed his finger toward Gérard Depardieu and simply said: "Saint Augustine!" The French actor was struck and later plunged into *The Confessions* by Saint Augustine. Fortunately. Soon he gave a public reading of selections from the work, which was immensely successful. Augustine had found himself a new friend with whom to open the third millennium.

Back in Rome. Eight years had passed. A white, frail silhouette walked to the front of the large Audience Hall, and the soft-spoken words of Benedict XVI quickly conveyed their compelling clarity:

> We too "find him alive" in his writings. When I read St. Augustine's writings, I do not get the impression that he is a man who died more or less 1,600 years ago; I feel he is like a man of today: a friend, a contemporary who speaks to me, who speaks to us with his fresh and timely faith. In St. Augustine who talks to us, talks to me in his writings, we see the everlasting timeliness of his faith; of the faith that comes from Christ, the Eternal Incarnate Word, Son of God and Son of Man. And we can see that this faith is not of the past although it was preached yesterday.[1]

[1] Benedict XVI, General Audience, January 16, 2008.

Benedict XVI and Gérard Depardieu, each in his own way, introduce us to the life of a saint who remains astonishingly contemporary, whose spirituality has come down through the centuries.

The purpose of the following pages is to help the reader to discover Saint Augustine, but also and above all to love him. Let us enter into his spirituality, let us draw water from a source that does not run dry, since it is so close to the Gospel of Christ.

PART ONE

# A SAINT FOR TODAY

A saint like Augustine is understood by his very life, and especially by his conversion, the indispensable key for entering into his thought and his spirituality. This is why we will quote extensively from his book *The Confessions*, a unique testimony in a literary genre unknown until then. In it, Augustine acknowledges his sins while confessing his faith in the merciful action of God. Let us not look at it as a personal journal but, rather, as a "sacrifice of praise and thanksgiving" to God the Savior. *The Confessions* are not so much an autobiography; they are dedicated to God, the master artisan and protagonist in Augustine's conversion.[1]

[1] Cf. G. Madec, *Le Dieu d'Augustin*, Philosophie et Théologie (Paris: Cerf, 2000), 86–89.

CHAPTER I

# Augustine, the African

## SUN AND SEA, WEALTH AND WOE

The year was 354. The blue waters of the Mediterranean played against the shores of Africa, glinting in the sun. That was where Augustine was born, amid the prosperity of North Africa at that time. Being far less dry than it is today and having assimilated the technology, institutions, and culture of Rome, North Africa was at that time a breadbasket of the Roman Empire.

Carthage and all of North Africa were an inspiration to poets and orators and an attraction for adventurers and the ambitious. To be in Carthage was the dream of many high-ranking Roman officials, much as today there are many who aspire to be an ambassador to Rome or London. Carthage was a symbol of easy living for the rich and a safe haven for students with grants and patrons. Everything about this beautiful city was attractive: it was open to maritime commerce and offered cultural activities such as the circus, the theater, and mime.

Before 313, the theater provided an opportunity to sully Christianity, while the circus was often soaked with the blood of martyrs. But now those practices had stopped, and the capital of Africa had become partly Christian. Nevertheless, during Augustine's time, Saint John Chrysostom remarked that many Christians knew the names of the charioteers and the numbers of the horses better than the names and number of the Apostles and prophets.[1] Less than ten years after Augustine's death, as the Vandals sowed terror throughout the continent, the bishop of Carthage, Quodvultdeus, wrote: "While the whole province is at death's door, crowds attend the spectacles every day; the blood is poured out daily on the earth, and the people cheer wildly every day in the circus."[2] Some months later, Carthage was stormed without difficulty by Genseric, king of the Vandals.

The students, whose studies had been paid for by grants or scholarships, lived in a world of privilege: the beauty of the sites and of the climate, the spectacles, and the intellectual life made Carthage a dream city for boisterous young men, whether they were trouble-makers or ambitious. Here, Augustine reported in his *Confessions*, they would heckle an instructor. These unruly youth vandalized the columns of a great library in Carthage with obscene graffiti.[3] Seven centuries before Augustine, Socrates had already said: "Our youth are poorly raised. They mock authority and have no respect at all for their elders. Our children today no longer rise

---

[1] Cf. Saint John Chrysostom, *Homilies on the Gospel of St. John*, Homily 58, 5.

[2] Quodvultdeus, sermon *De tempore barbarico*, in Marcel Neusch, *Initiation à saint Augustin. Maître spirituel* (Paris: Cerf, 1996), 251.

[3] Cf. A. G. Hamman, *La Vie quotidienne en Afrique du Nord au temps de saint Augustin* (Paris: Hachette, 1985), 114.

when their elders walk into the room, they talk back to their parents, and gossip instead of working. They are, quite simply, bad." There is nothing new under the sun.

Carthage, it must be said, was also home to terrible poverty, both material and moral. The Church had to support the poor, as local customs were stern and unforgiving. To the extent that he could, Augustine preached peace at Christmas time: "I am not asking you to fast. Eat, but do not become drunk. Do not behave as the pagans do. Show your good manners. Give food packages to the poor."[4]

The Roman Empire was immense and complex, hamstrung by an overgrown bureaucracy and crushing taxation. With their limited perspective, the masses could not see how this empire, which seemed unsinkable, had been weakened. Soon it would fall to the battering rams of the invaders.

Recall several important dates: Augustine was born in 354. When he celebrated his twentieth birthday, the Huns had already passed the Volga, driving back the Alemanni and Vandals in front of them. On August 24, 410, the Visigoths under Alaric invaded Rome. The Christians thought about the end times—had they arrived? No, Augustine would reply; the signs of the end times were not there. It was quite simply the empire that was in agony and, with it, a civilization. In 430, the Vandals besieged Hippo, where Augustine had remained, the pastor with his flock. That was where he died on August 28. Seven years later, Attila became ruler of the Huns.

---

[4] Saint Augustine, Sermon 198, 3.

Augustine was thus a man at the end of a civilization. But he would also become the architect of the birth of "Western Man", as Henri-Irénée Marrou evocatively puts it.

## A YOUNG MAN WITH AN OVERSIZED TALENT

Our saint was thus born in 354, in Thagaste, in modern-day Algeria. His father, Patricius, a pagan of the middle class, was the husband of Monica, a devout Christian and an attentive mother.

Very soon the parents noticed that their son was a gifted and persuasive child, and so did the friends who followed his lead. He learned quickly, even though he had to be compelled to study when he was very young. Augustine often spoke of his exceptional memory as a place of "spacious halls".[5] Very sensitive and shrewd, perhaps even emotional, he was interested in everything, absorbed everything, and quickly became remarkably cultured.

Augustine was a catechumen at this time. He had not yet been baptized, as was often the case in that era: many baptisms happened late, sometimes put off until the catechumen was near death. And so Augustine moved away from the God that Monica had tried to root in his heart. Many have exaggerated the antics of his youth, although they are true. Thus, in the famous episode of the stolen pears, no more was at stake than a few pieces of fruit in a very commonplace theft; but what Augustine describes

[5] Saint Augustine, *Confessions*, X, 8, 12.

is more profoundly the sin of evil done for its own sake. He "did not desire to enjoy what [he] stole, but only the theft and the sin itself."[6]

There was also the pleasure of vulgar and sensual stage performances. Writing in the *Confessions* about the circus games and the theater, he described this "voyeuristic" pleasure:

> Stage plays also captivated me, with their sights full of the images of my own miseries: fuel for my own fire. Now, why does a man like to be made sad by viewing doleful and tragic scenes, which he himself could not by any means endure? Yet, as a spectator, he wishes to experience from them a sense of grief, and in this very sense of grief his pleasure consists. What is this but wretched madness.[7] – Theaters, spectacles, lascivious love, obscene songs; such are the sweetness of concupiscence; sweet, indeed, and both savory and delectable.[8]

This young man lived with an attraction to beauty, to sensual pleasures, and with passion: "the thorn bushes of lust grew rank about my head.... I loved those inferior beauties, and I was sinking down to the very depths."[9] He cheated, stole, and lied, so sensuality became an obstacle to his conversion.

> The mists of passion ... dragged my unstable youth down over the cliffs of unchaste desires and plunged me into a gulf of infamy.... Where was I, and how far was I

[6] Ibid., II, 4, 9.
[7] Ibid., III, 2, 2.
[8] Saint Augustine, Sermon 153, 10.
[9] Saint Augustine, *Confessions*, II, 3, 6; IV, 13, 20.

exiled from the delights of your house, in that sixteenth
year of the age of my flesh, when the madness of lust
held full sway in me—that madness which grants indul-
gence to human shamelessness, even though it is forbidden by your laws—and I gave myself entirely to it?[10]

At the age of seventeen, he took a concubine, a common practice at the time. This union produced one child.
Fourteen years later, when Monica put a sorrowful end
to this relationship, Augustine, who had been faithful to
this woman, made a fresh start. "What afflicted me most
and what had made me already a slave to it was the habit
of satisfying an insatiable lust."[11]

Having a very sociable temperament, he developed
deep friendships. But these were not yet the friendships
"cemented" by charity. Instead, they were at the service
of his libertinism.

MEDITATE WITH SAINT AUGUSTINE:
THE THEFT OF THE PEARS

Saint Augustine describes in this passage the famous theft
of pears. In a subtle yet relentless analysis he shows the
capacity to do evil for the sake of evil, to practice trans-
gressions against the law:

Yet I had a desire to commit robbery, and did so, compelled to it by neither hunger nor poverty, but through
a contempt for well-doing and a strong impulse to

[10] Ibid., II, 2, 2 and 4.
[11] Ibid., VI, 12, 22.

iniquity.... I did not desire to enjoy what I stole, but only the theft and the sin itself.

There was a pear tree close to our own vineyard, heavily laden with fruit, which was not tempting either for its color or for its flavor. Late one night—having prolonged our games in the streets until then, as our bad habit was—a group of young scoundrels, and I among them, went to shake and rob this tree. We carried off a huge load of pears, not to eat ourselves, but to dump out to the hogs, after barely tasting some of them ourselves. Doing this pleased us all the more because it was forbidden.[12]

[12] Ibid., II, 4, 9.

# CHAPTER 2

# Toward Baptism

## FIRST CONVERSION

In 373, shortly after the birth of his son, Adeodatus, Augustine experienced his first conversion. When he discovered one of Cicero's works, *Hortensius* (which is lost today), he took an interest in the philosophical desire for truth. He was nineteen years old, and this set his heart on fire, in a real spiritual awakening. He made attempts to pray; his desires took on a noble character: "Every vain hope became worthless to me, and with an incredible warmth of heart I yearned for an immortality of wisdom."[1]

By reading this work, Augustine quite simply discovered the love of wisdom. Would the love of God be grafted onto this love? So many obstacles remained. Teaching in Thagaste and then in Carthage, his eloquence and knowledge shone forth. "During this period of nine years, from my nineteenth year to my twenty-eighth, I went astray and led others astray. I was deceived and deceived others, in varied lustful projects—sometimes publicly, by the teaching of what

---

[1] Saint Augustine, *Confessions*, III, 4, 7.

men style 'the liberal arts'; sometimes secretly, under the false guise of religion. In the one, I was proud of myself; in the other, superstitious; in all, vain!"[2]

His position teaching rhetoric in Carthage soon proved to be insufficient for him. In 383, he left to teach in Rome, then applied for a position in Milan. His ambition was immense. But toward what heights? "By the clamor of my own errors I was hurried outside myself, and by the weight of my own pride I was sinking ever lower.... I had my back toward the light."[3]

Nevertheless, reading the Scriptures still attracted him. As disconcerting as it may seem, his great pride made him despise the simple style. He did not let it touch his heart: "My inflated pride was repelled by their style, nor could the sharpness of my wit penetrate their inner meaning. Truly they were of a sort to aid the growth of little ones, but I scorned to be a little one and, swollen with pride, I looked upon myself as fully grown."[4]

## THE MANICHEAN ERROR

Note that Augustine was never an atheist or a follower of the gods of the Roman pantheon. He believed in God, but did not know where to anchor his confused belief: Who is God? How should he understand creation, man, and evil?

For about nine years, Augustine followed the path of Manichaeism. He was seduced by this sect, which he

[2] Ibid., IV, 1, 1.
[3] Ibid., IV, 15, 27, 30.
[4] Ibid., III, 5, 9. Saint Augustine, Sermon 51, 6.

contacted in Africa as early as 373. Some rather intelligent Manicheans captivated him in his quest. Moreover, Manichaeism allowed him to seek the truth "by pure and simple reason", and this flattered his pride. As Augustine himself puts it:

> For what else made me spurn, for nearly nine years, the religion that had been implanted in me from childhood by my parents and follow those men as an attentive disciple, if not their claim that we were overcome by a superstitious fear and were commanded to have faith before reason, but that they urge no one to have faith, without having first discussed and made clear the truth?...
> So I was when they found me, disdainful indeed of what seemed to me to be old wives' tales and desiring to grasp and to drink in the open, unadorned truth that they promised.[5]

The Manicheans also offered Augustine an answer to one of his burning issues, the question of evil. Their dualistic theory was based on a battle between two principles, two co-eternal substances: good and evil. The body is identified with evil, and the soul is itself twofold. One of the souls "being good and the other evil", the good soul was supposedly a particle of God, and the evil soul spawned by the race of darkness. How immensely advantageous this was for Augustine! The Manichean theory made him guiltless: "For it still seemed to me 'that it is not we who sin, but some other nature sinned in us.' And it gratified my pride to be beyond blame...."[6]

---

[5] Saint Augustine, *On the Profit of Believing*, I, 2.
[6] Saint Augustine, *Confessions*, V, 10, 18.

The Manichean life of "the perfect" or "the elect" was demanding (no marriage, no meat). But the life of the followers who were just "auditors" was much less so: "Those in their sect who are called auditors eat meat, till the ground, and take a wife if they want. But those whom they call the elect indulge in none of that."[7] There was another seductive element in that society which was imbued to some extent with Christian culture: the Manicheans give an honorable place to Scripture, but reinterpreted in their own way. They present themselves as "true Christians" in a superior form of Christianity that rejects the Old Testament as the work of the evil God.[8]

## HIS DAZZLING DISCOVERY OF PLATONISM

Ten years had passed since his discovery of Cicero. Augustine had gradually broken his ties with the Manicheans, because their solutions seemed to him too poor and elementary. Around 383, he encountered some academicians: skeptical philosophers. Their doctrine boiled down to the proposition "that we ought to doubt everything, ... that man does not have the power of comprehending any certain truth." Sequestering himself within these studies, he learned from them that "wisdom is not the truth itself, but the way that leads to it."[9] After this, he went through a period of doubts, skepticism, and

---

[7] Saint Augustine, Letter 236, 2.

[8] Saint Augustine, *Against Faustus*, I, 2–3.

[9] Saint Augustine, *Confessions*, V, 10, 19; Saint Augustine, *Against the Academicians*, I, 5, 14.

isolation. In this time of crisis, the God for whom he was groping was nevertheless at work in his heart.

Augustine left Carthage, where he said he could no longer stand the heckling of his students. He thought he would be better off in Rome, where the students were less noisy. Unfortunately, they proved to be dishonest and did not pay for their lessons. Aspiring to work in Milan, he competed successfully in 384 for a position as an official rhetorician at the imperial court. A professor of rhetoric, in those days, trained future officials of the empire there. The highest administrative offices were within Augustine's reach; at the age of thirty, he saw a brilliant future open to him. His meeting with the bishop of Milan, Ambrose, was critical, for the latter would gradually dispel his objections and draw him away from several errors. Nevertheless, our catechumen remained in a waiting position, still a prisoner of his carnal demons.

Augustine's contact with Neoplatonic works opened up new perspectives that were far less elementary than those of the Manicheans. He discovered Plotinus and Porphyry, and this reading kindled in him an "incredible fire".[10] He had left materialism behind, and these texts enlightened him, both on the nature of evil and on the spiritual reality of the soul. He learned to make a return toward "the interior of the self" and then, from

---

[10] Saint Augustine, *Against the Academicians*, II, 2, 5. Plotinus (died 270) and his pupil Porphyry (died ca. 300) are famous representatives of Plato's philosophy, which was very much alive at the time of Augustine. Augustine would be struck by their way of approaching the transcendence of the divine, beauty, the purification of the spirit, or interiority. Later on he would have to reconcile this thought with the Gospel.

that point, to God. He took an interest in contemplating a truth that is greater than just a search, a question. Something attractive that truly exists:

> And being admonished by these books to return into myself, I entered into my inward soul, guided by you. This I could do because you [were] my helper. And I entered, and with the eye of my soul—such as it was— saw above the same eye of my soul and above my mind the Immutable Light. It was not the common light, which all flesh can see.... He who knows the Truth knows that Light, and he who knows it knows eternity. Love knows it, O Eternal Truth and True Love and Beloved Eternity! You [are] my God, to whom I sigh both night and day.[11]

Jesus, the humble God, was still absent from his quest. The Platonists, by their contempt of the body, could not stomach a God made flesh. Moreover, these philosophers left Augustine in an attitude of pure intellectual superiority. He did not yet know how to listen and receive humbly, to believe in order to understand.

In this groping search, Providence put several intermediaries on his path who would guide him little by little toward the light. In order for God to reach the heart of man and instruct him, a "warning" is necessary. For as truth "warns without, it teaches within";[12] and through successive and varied mediations, God would give Augustine a sign and then teach him.

---

[11] Saint Augustine, *Confessions*, VII, 10, 16.
[12] Saint Augustine, *On Free Will*, II, 14, 38. Marcel Neusch, *Saint Augustin: Splendeur et misère de l'homme* (Paris: Cerf, 2011), 36–37.

## SAINT MONICA

What more could he owe his mother, Monica? Now a widow, she accompanied Augustine. In the battle that her son was waging, Monica fought with her weapons as a mother, ceaselessly praying for him with untiring fidelity. How many mothers have found in Monica a model! "For your hands, O my God, in the hidden design of your providence did not desert my soul; and out of the blood of my mother's heart, through the tears that she poured out by day and by night, there was a sacrifice offered to you for me."[13]

Her efforts call to mind Charles Journet's beautiful phrase: "Christ on the cross carried Monica, who carried Augustine." Indeed, Monica's prayerful mediation joined forces with the sacrifice of Jesus. One day, Monica confided her anguish to an African bishop, who then reassured her. Let us listen to Augustine: "When he had said this she was not satisfied, but repeated more earnestly her entreaties, and shed copious tears, still beseeching him to see and talk with me. Finally the bishop, a little vexed at her importunity, exclaimed, 'Go your way; as you live, it cannot be that the son of these tears should perish.' As she often told me afterward, she accepted this answer as though it were a voice from heaven."[14]

## SAINT AMBROSE

Let us not forget Saint Ambrose: he was one of the mediators for Augustine's conversion. In Milan, he was the

---

[13] Saint Augustine, *Confessions*, V, 7, 13.
[14] Ibid., III, 12, 21.

most important Catholic figure, one of immense influence. He had everything necessary to impress young Augustine: Ambrose came from the political aristocracy; his appointment as bishop, by acclamation of the people, had caused a great stir; and in a religious conflict, he had made Emperor Theodosius himself bend.

Augustine watched him and listened. He was captivated and often returned to listen to the pastor comment on Scripture, appreciating his oratory. In his confusion, he would have liked to consult Ambrose, but the latter was too busy to counsel Augustine. Well, there was still his preaching, and it would play an essential role: "By him I had been brought thus far to that wavering state of agitation I was now in, through which . . . I should pass from sickness to health, even though it would be after a still sharper convulsion which physicians call 'the crisis'." Crises are steps on the path to conversion.

Augustine learned to listen to the word of God. One of his friends gave him the Gospel of Saint John and the Letters of Saint Paul. This was not enough: "I restrained my heart from assenting to anything, fearing to fall headlong into error. Instead, by this hanging in suspense, I was being strangled."[15]

In particular, he lacked prayer: "Nor had I come yet to groan in my prayers that you [would] help me. My mind was wholly intent on knowledge and eager for disputation." Without the humility of heartfelt prayer, his approach remained primarily intellectual. The conversion of the will still tarried, and Augustine's account describes him in the worst distress, almost despairing

[15] Ibid., VI, 1, 1; 4, 6.

of finding the truth: "Where and when shall it be sought?... The winds of opinions veered about and tossed my heart hither and thither, time was slipping away. I delayed my conversion to the Lord; I postponed from day to day the life in you."[16]

He grew dismayed once more, as he began to glimpse the truth about himself, about his mediocrity in sin: "And I looked and I loathed myself; but whither to fly from myself I could not discover."[17] His first conscious cry for help, his first effective prayer, would occur in the garden of Milan, under the fig tree. God would answer it immediately.[18]

## "THE CONTAGION OF EXAMPLE"

In addition to his mother and a preaching bishop, God gave him other mediators. Serge Lancel quite rightly described them as the "contagion of example".[19] Thus, the old priest Simplicianus, Saint Ambrose's spiritual father, told Augustine about a striking conversion: Marius Victorinus was a famous rhetorician. Even during his lifetime, he had seen his own statue erected in the Roman Forum. He started to read the Scriptures and then converted to Catholicism. The impact was considerable. One can imagine how the proud Augustine could not help being moved: "The man of God had given me

[16] Ibid., VI, 3, 3; VI, 11, 18 and 20.
[17] Ibid., VIII, 7, 16.
[18] M. Dulaey, "Les Confessions", in *Connaissance des Pères de l'Église*, 55 (September 1994): 8.
[19] See S. Lancel, *Saint Augustin* (Paris: Fayard, 1999), 137.

this account of Victorinus, and I was already burning to imitate him." Nevertheless, Augustine hesitated:

> For this was what I was longing to do; but as yet I was bound by the iron chain of my own will. The enemy held fast my will, and had made of it a chain, and had bound me tight with it. For out of the perverse will came lust, and the service of lust ended in habit, and habit, not resisted, became necessity. By these links, as it were, forged together—which is why I called it "a chain"—a hard bondage held me in slavery.[20]

A few weeks later, Ponticianus, a Roman from Africa like Augustine, related to him news about other distressing conversions: two very high-ranking officials in the emperor's entourage had just listened to *The Life of Antony*, the famous Egyptian hermit. And then those two men met several monks, imitators of Antony's asceticism in simple huts. On the spot, they decided to leave everything, their offices, and even their fiancées to follow Christ. Augustine was distressed, but his soul "drew back. It refused. It would not make an effort. All its arguments were exhausted and confuted. Yet it resisted in sullen disquiet."[21]

At this stage of his conversion, experiences and examples were what moved Augustine far more than arguments. God acts through secondary causes ... and takes his time. An encounter with a tipsy tramp in the streets of Milan disturbed Augustine. The poor man's joy contrasted so much with his own sadness! Augustine asked

[20] Saint Augustine, *Confessions*, VIII, 5, 10.
[21] Ibid., VIII, 7, 18.

himself how he could "gain true joy".[22] Behind this
encounter was hidden the call of God.


## THE SUPREME MEDIATION:
## THE HUMBLE JESUS CHRIST

Augustine had to follow a path of humiliation in order
to renounce his pride, and this road passed through the
humble, incarnate Christ. Now, he had not found this
humble Christ Jesus among the Manicheans or the Neo-
platonists. "They do not know the way which is your
Word, by which you created all the things that are and
also the men who measure them.... For 'the Word was
made flesh' in order that your wisdom, by which you
created all things, might become milk for our infancy.
And, as yet, I was not humble enough to hold the humble Jesus; nor did I understand what lesson his weakness
was meant to teach us." [23]

Augustine would encounter Christ, a mediator for
us in the humility of the Incarnation and through the
abasement of the Cross. Augustine discovered that
God's initiative is rooted in the perfection of his infinite
love and mercy. Cicero fortunately had already taught
him the virtuous meaning of mercy. In praise of Caesar,
the great orator had exclaimed, "Among your virtues
none is more admirable and agreeable than your compassion."[24] The God "rich in mercy" of whom Saint

[22] Ibid., VI, 6, 9.
[23] Ibid., V, 3, 5; VII, 18, 24.
[24] Cited by Saint Augustine in *The City of God*, IX, 5.

Paul speaks (Eph 2:4) was revealed, little by little, in Christ's humility and weakness, instruments of salvation. Later, describing Jesus' walk to Jacob's well, Augustine would comment: "For it is not without a purpose that Jesus is weary; not indeed without a purpose that the strength of God is weary; not without a purpose that He is weary, by whom the wearied are refreshed ..., by whose absence we are wearied, by whose presence we are strengthened.... In [Christ's] weakness be strong, because what is 'the weakness of God is stronger than men.' "[25]

Yes, Christ was looking for Augustine; he sought him to heal him by his omnipotence. "His journey is the flesh assumed for love of us."[26] Christ's mercy would come to touch Augustine in the depths of his misery: "Lord, have pity on me.... Behold, I do not hide my wounds. You are the Physician, I am the sick man; you are merciful, I am miserable."[27]

One cannot understand Saint Augustine without grasping this essential trait. He lived his conversion as a profound experience, touching the root of his being. It was an experience of poverty and exchange with the strength of God, who, in order to reach him, became the humble and merciful Christ. "What mercy could surpass for the unfortunate the mercy that made the Creator of heaven descend from heaven; he condemned the True Bread to experience hunger, Fullness to have

---

[25] Saint Augustine, *Homilies on the Gospel of St. John*, XV, 6–7 [*Nicene and Post-Nicene Fathers*, First Series, ed. Philip Schaff (Peabody, Mass.: Hendrickson, 1995; hereafter abbreviated NPNF), 7:100b–101a].

[26] Ibid.

[27] Saint Augustine, *Confessions*, X, 28, 39.

thirst, reduced Power to weakness, Holiness to suffering, Life to death; and he did this to still our hunger, to
quench our thirst, to relieve our sufferings, to extinguish
iniquity, and to inflame charity."[28]

Commenting on the episode of the adulterous woman
(Jn 8:1–11), Augustine offers an explanation that sounds
like a self-portrait. The scene is well known: one by one,
the guilty woman's accusers have left. "The two were
left alone: the wretched woman and Mercy."[29] *Misera
et misericordia.* These two words sum up an encounter
and resound like a cry of hope for salvation. Augustine,
confronted with Christ, had to take the step of humility, but also to beg for this virtue through prayer. The
word of God would play a decisive role, through the
writings of Saint Paul.


IN THE GARDEN OF MILAN

As we have said, Augustine did not think of surrendering
or of asking God for help. He suffered in this "struggle of
myself against myself", which seemed doomed to failure:
"Yet I still did not quite reach or touch or grasp the goal,
because I hesitated to die to death and to live to life. And
the worse way, to which I was habituated, was stronger in
me than the better, which I had not tried."[30]

Here, finally, was the moment when moaning became
prayer, when desire began to beseech. Grace would be
given to this soul finally open to the word of God. In
the summer of 386, Augustine was standing in a garden

[28] Saint Augustine, Sermon 207, 1.
[29] Saint Augustine, *Homilies on the Gospel of St. John*, XXXIII, 5.
[30] Saint Augustine, *Confessions*, VIII, 11, 25.

in Milan with his friend Alypius. He stepped aside a little. The presence of a friend became useless to him, even unbearable. Upset and not knowing what to do, he wept, and finally he prayed: " 'Why not now? Why not this very hour make an end to my uncleanness?' I was saying these things and weeping in the most bitter contrition of my heart, when suddenly I heard the voice of a boy or a girl—I know not which—coming from the neighboring house, chanting over and over again, 'Pick it up, read it; *tolle, lege!*' "

He returned to Alypius, grabbed a book of Saint Paul's writings, and read: "Not in reveling and drunkenness; not in debauchery and licentiousness, not in quarreling and jealousy. But put on the Lord Jesus Christ, and make no provision for the flesh, to gratify its desires" (Rom 13:13–14). "I wanted to read no further, nor did I need to. For instantly, as the sentence ended, there was infused in my heart something like the light of full certainty and all the gloom of doubt vanished away."[31] In this garden of re-creation, Augustine had found the tree of life thanks to the effective, transforming word of God.

From then on, events followed one another rapidly, in that certainty which would never again abandon Augustine. He prepared for baptism. At the Easter vigil, April 24, 387, Augustine was baptized together with his son, Adeodatus, and his friend, Alypius, at the hands of Ambrose himself. He was thirty-three years old. At the age when Christ died, Augustine was born into the light through baptism: "The Lord draws the dead man from the grave, he it is who touches the heart." He shouted

---

[31] Ibid., VIII, 12, 28–29.

his joy in God's gift, the gift of life: "But our very Life came down to earth and bore our death, and slew it with the very abundance of his own life."[32]


CONVERSION: SPIRITUAL EVENT
AND GIFT OF GOD


What a winding road! Augustine had had to experience the deep dissatisfaction of his heart in order to find at last the peace of God. His conversion was a total change of mentality, a repentance: a *metanoia*. It was also a turning back to God, whom he discovered present in his heart. It was a moral event, an upheaval of his intellect and will. It was a gift, a grace, without hindering his freedom. The desire to believe, the first prayer ... all this was grace. Even the sadness that accompanies repentance is also a pure gift of God.[33]

The encounter with the merciful face of Jesus Christ, the incarnate and humble Word, is the heart of conversion. This experience touched the deepest part of his being and forever shaped the "I" of Augustine, which is constituted in the presence of the "Thou" of God made man. The encounter happened, not through a fusion of man into the Plotinian One (a philosophical temptation with which Augustine had flirted, whereby contact with the One "evaporates" the personality, to the point that the believer loses all notion of self), but rather in an encounter with a person: Christ Jesus.

---

[32] Saint Augustine, Sermon 295; Saint Augustine, *Confessions*, IV, 12, 19.

[33] "For your sin, the very thing that gave you displeasure, would not have displeased you unless God's light had illumined you" (Saint Augustine, *Homilies on the Gospel of St. John*, XII, 13).

Augustine left "the region of unlikeness" where man is exiled by his sin, like another Adam far from paradise. An exile far from oneself and an imbalance of one's deepest being, far from the interior life that is peace and equilibrium. Augustine, in a certain sense, was recreated by Scripture and by the grace of his conversion. Through his baptism, the likeness of Christ was imprinted upon him: the *forma omnium*, the form of all things, the model of all re-creation and the perfect image.[34]

Augustine was definitively marked by this experience of living mercy, Jesus Christ himself. His theological work, his pastoral activity, and even his style would be imbued with a characteristic "cordiality". Mercy became a key to understanding, to "knowing in love".

It was a single event, leading to definitive certitudes. And yet conversion, which is never completed, would require Augustine to make new renunciations. Although he experienced a *Pascha*—literally a "passage" of death to sin and of resurrection—other sacrifices would still be required of him.

MEDITATE WITH SAINT AUGUSTINE:
THE JOY OF CONVERSION

Augustine converted in the garden of Milan. Free at last and joyful, he sang his thanksgiving:

"O Lord, I am your servant; I am your servant and the son of your handmaid. You have loosed my bonds.

[34] M.-A. Vannier, *Saint Augustin: La conversion en acte* (Paris: Entrelacs, 2011), 96.

I will offer to you the sacrifice of thanksgiving." Let my heart and my tongue praise you, and let all of my bones say, "Lord, who is like unto you?" Let them say so, and answer me and say to my soul, "I am your salvation." . . .

How sweet did it suddenly become to me to be without the sweetness of trifles! And it was now a joy to put away what I formerly feared to lose. For you cast them away from me, O true and highest Sweetness. You cast them away, and in their place you yourself entered in—sweeter than all pleasure, though not to flesh and blood; brighter than all light, but more veiled than all mystery; more exalted than all honor, though not to them that are exalted in their own eyes.

Now was my soul free from the gnawing cares of seeking and getting, of wallowing in the mire and scratching the itch of lust. And I prattled like a child to you, O Lord my God—my light, my riches, and my salvation.[35]

[35] Saint Augustine, *Confessions*, IX, 1, 1.

CHAPTER 3

# The Man "Consumed" by His
# Pastoral Duties (391–430)

## A PRIEST "IN SPITE OF HIMSELF"

Between his conversion in the garden in Milan and his baptism, Augustine had created a little community on the rural property of a friend in Cassiciacum, not far from the great imperial city. From his exchanges of a rather philosophical nature, in which Adeodatus and sometimes Monica participated, arose writings in the form of dialogues (*Against the Academicians, The Happy Life,* among others). They prayed together, and Augustine, following Ambrose's advice, was nourished by the word of God. In this way, he returned to his heart, then went out of himself toward God and from God toward his neighbor, in community life.

In September 387, Augustine and his family left Milan to go to Africa. But Monica died in Ostia, not far from Rome; she was fifty-six years old. Augustine confides his grief to us and reports in his *Confessions* the conversation that he had with her several days before her death. He describes a form of ecstasy and the extraordinary union of souls of a son with his mother, as few others have experienced it.

> We were conversing alone very pleasantly and "forget-
> ting those things which are past, and reaching forward
> toward those things which are future." We were in the
> ... presence of Truth, which you are[, O Lord]....
> We soared higher yet by an inner musing, speaking
> and marveling at your works. And we came at last to
> our own minds and went beyond them, that we might
> climb as high as that region of unfailing plenty where
> you feed Israel forever with the food of truth, where life
> is that Wisdom by whom all things are made.[1]

Upon his return to Africa, Augustine founded a little monastery with his friends. From then on, he dedicated his life entirely to reflection, to the contemplation of the beauty and truth of the word of God. Three happy years were spent in this way, during which Augustine thought that he had reached the goal of his life, in communal peace and unity.

The year 391 upset everything. Augustine traveled to the port city of Hippo to meet there a friend whom he hoped to recruit to the monastic life. Until then, he had successfully avoided the towns without bishops: he feared the priesthood and the pastoral responsibility of that office. There might be a repeat of Ambrose's experience. Now it happened that during the Sunday liturgy at the cathedral in which he was participating, someone recognized him. Augustine did not know that the bishop, Valerius, had publicly expressed the desire to ordain a

[1] Saint Augustine, *Confessions*, IX, 10, 23–24.

priest who could take on the job of preaching. This was because Valerius, being of Greek origin, did not speak Latin well, much less Punic, and he preached only with difficulty. Immediately those in attendance pointed out Augustine. They forced him to present himself to be ordained a priest. He wept and suffered, but Augustine obeyed. His beautiful dream of contemplative life faded, and his life was upended; he asked for three months of diaconate in order to prepare for the priesthood and to study. . . .

Immediately after his "forced" ordination, Augustine wrote to his bishop, Valerius: "I felt like someone who did not even know how to handle an oar yet was assigned to second place at the helm. . . . This explains the tears which some of my brethren saw me shedding in the city at the time of my ordination."[2]


THE MAN "CONSUMED":
A "SECOND CONVERSION"


It all went very fast. Augustine was consecrated Valerius' coadjutor bishop in 395, then succeeded him the following year. From then on, he had to live with Christ, but for others, and to translate his knowledge into the thought and the language of the simple folk of his city. The great philosophical work of a lifetime that he dreamed of would remain unwritten. Instead, he left us something else: the Gospel translated into the language of the people. And is that not even more valuable?

---

[2] Saint Augustine, Letter 21, 1–2.

Augustine describes as follows what would hereafter be his daily routine:

> I learned how I must live. What need do I have to render an accounting for the lives of others? But the Gospel fills me with dread.... Constant preaching, arguing, reprimanding, edifying, being available to everyone: this is a considerable responsibility, a heavy burden, an endless difficulty.... We have to reprimand the undisciplined, console the faint-hearted, support the weak, refute the opponents, be wary of the clever, instruct the ignorant, stir up the lazy, thwart the belligerent, restrain the proud, appease the quarreling, help the needy, liberate the oppressed, encourage the good, tolerate the wicked, and love everyone.[3]

Who would not try to shirk this task? Yes, Augustine was tempted to flee, but he stood fast and remained faithful to his responsibility. This was a new "conversion" to which Benedict XVI refers: "This was the second conversion which this man, struggling and suffering, was constantly obliged to make: to be available to everyone, time and again, and not for his own perfection; time and again, to lay down his life with Christ so that others might find him, true Life."[4] This forty-two-year-old man renounced tranquility so as to devote himself to his people.

Like the bishops of his time, he had to administer justice, preside at the tribunal of civil cases for the Christians. His biographer Possidius reports that "he

---

[3] Saint Augustine, Sermon 339, 4; then 340, 1.
[4] Benedict XVI, Homily in Pavia, April 22, 2007; May 20, 2007.

ceaselessly heard and decided cases, sometimes until the hour of the midday meal; but sometimes, too, for the whole day, without eating, he turned his attention to the deep motives of these Christian hearts."[5] He also interceded for the guilty, took care of the sick and the abandoned. How burdensome this administrative duty was for him! He admits it: "I take God as my witness that all this administration of temporal goods is a burden on me. It is for me a form of servitude that I endure out of fear of the Lord and charity for my brethren."[6]

All this often obsessed him and, of course, exhausted him. Hippo, which was called a "royal" city in antiquity, was not an obscure seaside village; it was the second largest city on the coast of North Africa, after Carthage, a city whose bishop, Aurelius, developed a very strong bond with Augustine. The two of them would be organizers of African ecclesiastical life. During that era of schisms and incipient heresies, Augustine would be hard at work, without respite. His renown quickly spread beyond Africa, and correspondents wrote to the bishop of Hippo from all over the empire. He felt obliged to respond, all the more because his sense of friendship prompted him to cultivate these exchanges: "If I could tell you all the hours of my days and nights that I must devote to the needs of others, you would find it staggering, and you would be surprised by the multitude of affairs that prevent me from dedicating myself to the writing that you request of me, and I regret that I cannot resume it."[7]

[5] Possidius, *Vie*, 19.
[6] Saint Augustine, Letter 226, 9, and Letter 139, 2.
[7] Saint Augustine, Letter 139, 3.

His theological works suffered as a result. He wrote during much of the night, and it would take him almost twenty years to compose his *Treatise on the Trinity*. Not only did he have to carry "the burden of life", like everyone else, but he also carried on his shoulders his *sarcina*, the weight of his "pack": "At the moment I am speaking to you about a burden; what is it but you yourselves?"[8] However, he never says "You are my flock", but rather he says: "You are God's flock." The real look-out of the ship is not he, the bishop, but the one Shepherd who sees and looks into the heart of each one.

He ceaselessly repeated to his faithful: "While they do imitate the works of the good shepherds, the good sheep do not place their hopes in those whose minis-try gathers them, but rather in the Lord whose blood redeems them."[9] One passage admirably reflects this teaching about the pastor-servant. How could we not find Augustine himself in it when he mentions the Apostle Peter?

Although he proved his fear by denying the Shepherd, let him prove his love by feeding the Lord's flock. Those whose purpose in feeding the flock of Christ is to have them as their own, and not as Christ's, are by that very fact convicted of loving themselves, and not Christ.... For what do these words mean, "Do you love me? Feed my sheep"? Is it not to say: If you love me, do not think of feeding yourself, but feed my sheep, and do not feed them as your own, but as mine.[10]

---

[8] Saint Augustine, Sermon 340, 1.
[9] Saint Augustine, Letter 208, 6; cf. Saint Augustine, Sermon 340, 1.
[10] Saint Augustine, *Homilies on the Gospel of St. John*, 123, 4–5.

Augustine lived out this doctrine throughout his life, which he offered and gave as a *servitium amoris*, a service of love.

## BISHOP AND MONK: "ORDINARY" HOLINESS?

Having become a "bishop in spite of himself", Augustine remained "a monk despite everything", as André Mandouze writes.[11] When Bishop Valerius called him to be his assistant, Augustine had been able to get permission to gather brothers in a house at the back of a garden. That was an initial monastery. After living there for several years, he was consecrated a bishop and soon replaced Valerius. He then founded in his episcopal residence another monastery with his clergy. The bishop wanted to live in the midst of his confreres.

Augustine intended to harmonize action and contemplation. In his view, pastoral charity was the only justification for leaving prayer and theological study: "Our motive for becoming involved in activity should be the charity of necessity, so that if no one imposes this burden on us, we must devote ourselves to seeking and contemplating the truth.... And even then we must not abandon altogether the sweetness of contemplation."[12]

Moreover, he continued to have an acute sense of the poverty that he desired for all his priests who were gathered around him in the episcopal residence. More

---

[11] A. Mandouze, *Saint Augustin: L'aventure de la raison et de la grâce* (Paris: Éditions augustiniennes, 1968), 166ff.

[12] Saint Augustine, *The City of God*, XIX, 19.

than anyone else, he could dispense with the pomp that
so many bishops dreamed about. For example, if someone offered him a precious garment, he would reply,
"Maybe it suits the bishop, but it does not suit Augustine, a poor man."[13]

Nietzsche said one day that he could not stand Saint
Augustine, whom he considered so ordinary. He would
have preferred it if the pastor of Hippo had been merely
an intellectual aristocrat. But the latter became a pastor, a servant of God's faithful, wedding himself to the
everyday cares of those men and women.

As Joseph Ratzinger (Benedict XVI) wrote, Augustine "became increasingly an ordinary man among
ordinary men and the servant of all. In the process, he
became truly a saint. Christian holiness does not consist
in being somehow superhuman or in having outstand-
ing talents or a stature that someone else does not have.
Christian holiness is simply the obedience that makes us
available where God calls us to be, the obedience that
does not rely on our own greatness but allows our God
to bestow his greatness on us."[14] Augustine, our brother
in humanity, leads us toward the heights.

## FINAL STAGES IN HUMILITY AND
## RENUNCIATION (427–430)

Let us then follow Augustine again in his ascent. Around
the year 427, the aging bishop composed a book of

[13] Saint Augustine, Sermon 356, 13.
[14] Joseph Ratzinger, *Dogma and Preaching*, trans. Michael J. Miller and Matthew J. O'Connell (San Francisco: Ignatius Press, 2011), 367.

*Retractions*, in which he reviewed the works that he had written, noting critiques and corrections. Few authors have had the intellectual humility to apply their mind to such a critical review of their own work.

When he was young, Augustine thought that sanctity could attain here on earth such a degree of perfection that the words of the Gospel would apply without reservation: "It is not by measure that [God] gives the Spirit" (Jn 3:34). The pilgrim on the holy mountain of sanctity could claim to be "perfect" here below. He corrected this idea: "I had not understood that this passage truly applied only to Jesus Christ."[15] At this stage of his life, Augustine advanced more profoundly on the paths of mercy and humility, without ever weakening with regard to the demands of his office as bishop.[16]

Saint Augustine blamed himself also for having described man as desiring to live a happy life by perfecting himself in terms of his greatest human feature: reason, the mind. Rather, man should live according to God's commands in order to arrive at happiness, he observes, and man finds his supreme happiness, not in himself, but on God's terms and in God: "In order to arrive at this happiness, our soul must not be content with itself, it must submit to God."[17]

The humility of the learned doctor would be reinforced by the renunciation of the pastor: "It is more fitting that we should follow God's will than that he

[15] Saint Augustine, *Retractions*, I, 19, 3.
[16] See Benedict XVI, Homily in Pavia, April 22, 2007.
[17] Saint Augustine, *Retractions*, I, 1, 2, referring to Saint Augustine, *Against the Academicians*, I, 2, 5.

should follow ours.... The true plan of action is to resolve never to fight against God's power."[18]

Augustine had the prospect of renunciation of this sort in the twilight of his life, on the occasion of a terribly painful trial. The Vandals had invaded Africa and were devastating the region. Everything about Catholicism that he had built up—the communities, the catechized faithful, the unity that had been reestablished—could very well be destroyed. But Augustine was unwilling to flee; the bishop did not want to abandon his people. "Our ministry is so necessary for them that they must not be deprived of it. There is nothing else for us to do, then, but to say to the Lord: be our God, our protector, and our place of refuge."[19]

Relying on God, he gave the ultimate proof of love and detachment: remaining with his own people, taking charge of them, even to the end. "Obviously, those who are able to escape from such evils by fleeing yet prefer to remain and not abandon their brethren in distress give the highest proof of charity."[20]

Perfection consists of this gift of love; Augustine thus shows the perfection of self-abandonment, filled with faith, love of God's will, and hope for the future.

Augustine fell ill; on August 28, 430, in Hippo, he breathed his last, almost sixty-six years old. The Roman provinces of Africa were invaded by the Vandals, and the empire collapsed. For Augustine, this was the hour of the long-desired encounter, while his written work would survive him and his example would go down through the centuries. Augustine remains alive.

[18] Saint Augustine, *Catechism of the Uninstructed*, 14, 20.
[19] Possidius, *Vie*, 30, 4–5.
[20] Saint Augustine, Letter 228, 3.

MEDITATE WITH SAINT AUGUSTINE:
THE BISHOP, THE GOOD SHEPHERD,
MODELED ON SAINT PETER

Saint Peter, on Mount Tabor, would have liked to enjoy
the peace that the Transfiguration of Jesus brought.
He was called to descend "into the valley" in order
to devote himself to his apostolate until death. In this
homily, Augustine describes his own life, too. A pastor's
asceticism is to accept labors, to work unceasingly, to
wear himself out for the benefit of his people.

Descend, Peter; you wanted to rest on the mountain
[of the Transfiguration]; go down, preach the word, be
urgent in season and out of season; convince, rebuke,
and exhort, be unfailing in patience and in teaching;
work, sweat, suffer torments so that through the bright-
ness and beauty of good works performed with charity,
you come to possess what the Lord's white garments
symbolize.... Peter did not yet understand this when
he wanted to remain with Christ on the mountain. O
Peter, Christ reserved this happiness for you after death.
For now he tells you: go down and work on earth, serve
on earth, and on earth be handed over to contempt and
the cross. Did not Life itself descend to undergo death,
the Bread—to endure hunger, the Way—to become
weary of walking, the eternal Fountain—to suffer
thirst? And you refuse to work? Do not seek your own
interest. Have charity, proclaim the truth, and so you
will arrive at the unchangeable peace of eternity.[21]

---

[21] Saint Augustine, Sermon 78, 6.

# CHAPTER 4

# Fruitfulness in Time

## AN IMMENSE THEOLOGICAL
## AND SPIRITUAL HERITAGE

Augustine died. The African soil was strewn with heaps of ruins. Still, the bishop's thought kept spreading, beyond Hippo and soon beyond his century. Even during his lifetime, Saint Jerome had saluted him as "the restorer of the ancient faith"; his manuscripts circulated, and they were copied, sometimes even before the intended recipient was acquainted with them. . . .

Only nine months after his death, Pope Celestine paid tribute to Augustine as one "of the greatest teachers". The figure of the bishop of Hippo dominated not only the theology but also the thought and literature of the Latin West. Alongside him, other names pale a bit. His works were quoted, annotated, studied, and plagiarized. Because his readers admired him. Pope Gregory the Great described that "aura" using an agricultural metaphor: "Beware of preferring our bran to this pure wheat."

One remark must be made, however: Augustine did nothing but profess the Catholic Creed; he had no other purpose than to defend it against heresies, to comment on it for his faithful or his correspondents. He intended neither to set a spiritual or theological trend, nor even to demonstrate his originality. Yet this man had written so much, debated so much, spoken so much (eight thousand homilies or even more), that with his genius he had encompassed large swaths of the Gospel heritage, but also of Latin culture. His profound and universal thought brought precision and clarity to many topics of Catholic doctrine that were still confused in the minds of many. Sometimes his formulations would become fixed points of reference for the Magisterium. And so he is, indeed, the "Doctor of grace", since he so ardently defended this grace of God without which man does no good. Considering the theology of the sacraments and of the Church, Father Congar concludes that Augustine "rethought the whole problem of the Church and of the sacraments in a coherent system. Moreover, he was not content to refute, to combat, and to reduce the schism; he taught positively, and his teaching was for the most part incorporated into the development of Catholic dogma."[1]

On other more particular points, his theses were not retained by Church tradition. Some of these appear in his youthful works; the bishop's thought, however, was able to advance farther: "Why does anyone seek what he knows to be incomprehensible, unless because one must never cease to investigate incomprehensible things as long as it is profitable, and one becomes better and

[1] Yves Congar, "Introduction générale" to the Traités anti-donatistes, I, BA 28 (1963), 80–81.

better at seeking such a great good, which is always to be found when one seeks it, and always to be sought when one finds it."[2] Moreover, Augustine the rhetorician could be very harsh in polemical debates. He knew how to make a point. Taken out of context, some formulations sound outrageous. An isolated topic, which arose in a polemical situation, can lead a commentator into error.

## SAINT AUGUSTINE AND SAINT THOMAS

The medieval theologians forged their spiritual theology by relying on the genius of Augustine, who centuries earlier had laid the foundations for it with multiple reflections. Among the greatest are Anselm of Canterbury, Bernard of Clairvaux, Hugh of Saint Victor, and the other Victorine canons. Or even Peter Lombard, Thomas Aquinas, and Bonaventure.

When theology soared to new heights in the mid-eleventh century, Augustine was again the source of the principles and materials used to build the cathedral of knowledge. But with the return of Aristotle in thirteenth-century Scholasticism, Augustine's place changed. In a way, some set up another teacher against him. Saint Thomas would be able to make a true synthesis by relying on these two geniuses.

Saint Augustine's method of reflection is original. His desire for wisdom drives him to view reality as a whole rather than to consider just one part or one aspect of

---

[2] Saint Augustine, *On the Trinity*, XV, 2, 2.

things. For each question, Augustinian thought gathers the elements from different known fields into a unified, dynamic, and concrete meditation. Thus, when Saint Augustine reflected on the human condition, he considered at the same time "human nature", the actual state of sinful man, salvation through Christ, or the promises of eternal life, etc. This process of unification is not always clear to our minds, which have been shaped by the habit of making distinctions and divisions. This sometimes makes reading Saint Augustine difficult.

It should be noted also that the deviant interpretations of the Augustinian corpus appeared precisely in the eras of major conceptual specialization. In other words, the unity of the Augustinian view is not only profound and bracing, but also sure and prudent. It is a form of wisdom.

Some writers, then, would like to set Augustine and Thomas Aquinas in opposition because they employ different methods. But how can you compare the African bishop from the fourth and fifth centuries with this Scholastic from the thirteenth? Augustine is, in the first place, a pastor, and Thomas—a professor; the contrast is between "a fisher of men and a builder of truths", as Jacques Maritain wrote, concluding at the end of a fine study: "We must say ... that, by means of a general transposition and many slight adjustments that are required as a result, the whole substance of the Augustinian doctrine of the truth was carried over into the writings of Saint Thomas."[3]

---

[3] Jacques Maritain, *Distinguier pour unir ou les Degrés du savoir* (Paris: Desclée de Brouwer, 1947), 606.

It is not difficult to count the positions on which Augustine and Thomas differ; but it is impossible to enumerate those on which they agree.

## THE RENAISSANCE AND THE REFORMATION

Through the theologians of the Augustinian Order (canons regular and hermits of Saint Augustine) and the Franciscan School, Augustine's heritage remained fruitful until the end of the Middle Ages, although it is different from what is offered in Thomism in the writings of the successors of Thomas Aquinas.

What happened during the Renaissance? In the battles and imbalances of Christendom and in intellectual history itself, Augustine was enlisted by parties that were sometimes in opposition. The humanists returned to antiquity and the Fathers of the Church; they gladly rediscovered Augustine. A renewal of Platonism and an anti-Aristotelian reaction contributed to this, too. Half of the printed works that appeared before 1500—the incunabula—are works by Saint Augustine (or attributed to our Doctor).

At the time of the Protestant Reformation, the question about a Christian's justification became more pointed in theological debate. Both Luther and Calvin thought that Catholicism taught a form of practical Pelagianism, in which God's grace was not absolutely necessary. They insisted on original sin, concupiscence, and the radical weakness of man without grace, the salvation that comes from God. In this regard, the Reformers often invoked the authority of Augustine. Now, at the same time, the Catholic Counter-Reformation and some theologians from various religious orders also relied on the teaching of the bishop of Hippo, while giving a less pessimistic, more nuanced interpretation. A genius like Augustine could not help but have so many and such diverse intellectual descendants that we cannot fairly claim that he endorses all these interpretations.

## THE SEVENTEENTH CENTURY, "SAINT AUGUSTINE'S CENTURY"

This expression used by Jean Dagens is meant to sum up the extraordinary attraction that Augustine exerted on that period, especially in France. Thus, Cardinal Bérulle, who was able to emphasize the humility of Augustinian spirituality. Or Jean-Jacques Olier, too, who writes: "After the sacred books, I think that those by the great Saint Augustine are infinitely above all the rest." We know what a great influence this founder of seminaries would have in the formation of priests. Moreover, the Oratory of France, founded in 1613, claims to be rooted in the spirit of Saint Augustine. As for Bossuet, we owe to him this fine praise of Augustine: "My God, make me think what he thought, make me know what he knew, make me believe what he believed, make me preach what he preached."

Unfortunately, we cannot conceal the long quarrel of Jansenism, which started with the book by Jansenius, bishop of Ypres, entitled *Augustinus*. The doctrine on grace is at issue here. In it Jansen's adversaries—among them many Jesuits—saw theses deserving condemnation:

for instance, that predestination concerned not only the elect but also the damned—which would be terrifying. Augustine is summoned as a witness to support each camp. This time again, people forgot that Augustine's thought evolved and ultimately placed the accent on God's mercy and patience. In response to this pessimistic Jansenist current, other authors fortunately became the interpreters of a less caricatured Augustine. But the tragedy would obscure his image for a long time.[4]

## AUGUSTINE AND HIS INFLUENCE IN RELIGIOUS LIFE

Saint Augustine—and later some African bishops, his disciples—founded monasteries for men and women, giving them a rule about which we will speak later on. Different versions of it crossed the Mediterranean and influenced several religious foundations in the West. Thus, the great Saint Benedict adapted "several of its best formulas" or was freely inspired by it.[5] The objective of a united community and an attentive superior who adapts to each member took shape in this Benedictine Rule, which went on to irrigate all of Latin monasticism.

The canonial movement—uniting common life and liturgical life, contemplation and apostolate within the

---

[4] Concerning these two paragraphs, compare the summary given by B. Boisson, *Saint Augustin: Le bonheur d'être chrétien* (Nouan-le-Fuzelier: EDB, 2016), 67–69.

[5] Cf. A. de Vogüé, *La Règle de saint Benoît*, Sources chrétiennes 181 (Paris: Cerf, 1972), 33–39; 279ff.

framework of a local church—took flight prodigiously in the eleventh and twelfth centuries, numbering no less than two thousand monasteries in Europe and the Near East. Some clerical religious communities adopted this rule, in the shadow of the cathedrals, collegiate churches, or shrines. In the female version, canonesses are contemplative or apostolic (Norbertine nuns, canonesses of Latran, of Saint Victor, or of Windesheim, nursing Sisters of Mercy, teaching Sisters of Notre Dame, and others). Although they were uprooted and driven out of France after the Revolution, canonesses and canons regular are reviving today.

Let us not forget that Saint Dominic was a canon regular; he intended to keep the Augustinian Rule for the community of nuns that he founded in 1206, then for his preaching friars. From the thirteenth century on, most orders of hospitallers, later of clerics regular, and dozens of female communities adopted this rule. Because of its flexibility and sobriety, in the context of a Church that wants to limit the number of rules, it was chosen by several hundred institutes.

In another development, diverse communities living under the Rule of Saint Augustine gave rise to an organization that would be called—in the broad sense—the Order of Saint Augustine. The Middle Ages witnessed the flourishing of around two thousand convents, with thirty thousand religious, who were also called Hermits of Saint Augustine. In the modern era, throughout the world, we see it in the missions, education, care for the sick and the poor, and finally in study and research, because the order includes great theologians. Like the canons regular, their community life appears in the feminine form, also, in all fields of charitable work! In the nineteenth century, "the group of the Assumption was the most spectacular proof of the new growth of the old Augustinian tree."[6] Father d'Alzon founded the Assumptionists, who carry on an apostolate of teaching, mission work, ecclesial unity, and Catholic publishing (for example, the French newspaper La Croix). Under the patronage of Our Lady of the Assumption, several institutes reprise the Augustinian spirit in a feminine key.

Augustine's influence extends beyond those who live by his rule, almost everywhere but to various degrees. Thus, Saint Bonaventure and the major current of medieval Franciscan theology do not hide their debt to Augustine.

In the sixteenth and seventeenth centuries, in the spiritual renewal that went through Christendom, the religious were privileged agents, and Augustine exerted a great influence among them. In the Carmelite Order, the reformer Teresa of Ávila was enthusiastic about the Confessions of Augustine. Some important elements of Augustinian spirituality can be found in the writings of La Madre. Let us mention only the remark from the Soliloquies, "Let me know myself, that I may know you", or the "return to the heart" through interiorization, which would give an Augustinian flavor to the spiritual doctrine that Teresa bequeathed to the Carmelites.[7] Three centuries later, the teaching of Thérèse

---

[6] M. Cocheril, "L'ordre canonial", in G. Le Bras, ed., Les Ordres religieux, vol. 2 (Paris: Flammarion, 1980), 132.

[7] See, for example, J.-Ph. Houdret, "L'influence de saint Augustin sur sainte Thérèse d'Avila", Vives Flammes 174 (1988/5): 33–43.

of Lisieux preserves strong Augustinian accents, to the point where some could say that she lived in an "Augustinian element". There is nothing exceptional about this in the nineteenth century, but it certainly contributes toward a spirituality of mercy or of the primacy of charity in the writings of this very young Doctor of the Church.

## CULTURAL INFLUENCE

Augustine's intellectual breadth explains, moreover, a fruitfulness that goes beyond theology and spirituality. A man as steeped in erudition as the Protestant Adolf von Harnack boldly wrote: "All the great personalities who recreated a new life in the Western Church or purified and deepened its piety issued directly or indirectly from Saint Augustine and were formed in his school."

Countless religious, philosophers, theologians, psychologists, preachers, writers, and mystics drew from this source. There are so many from the sixteenth and seventeenth centuries whose names we would like to mention—La Bruyère, Malebranche, and no doubt Descartes—who would have a lasting influence on the interpretations given to the teaching of the bishop of Hippo. As for the world of science, how many people know that the famous Gregor Mendel, who discovered the laws of heredity, was an Augustinian monk?

In a recent book, Jean-François Petit shows that throughout the twentieth century "Western man is often 'Augustinian' without knowing it ... [and that] in reality a great many questions are worked through with

Augustine."[8] In fact, what variety there is among his heirs! And sometimes what divergent views! Heidegger, Laberthonnière, Gadamer, Arendt, Landsberg, Jaspers, Mounier, Camus, Derrida, Ricoeur, Lyotard, Marion, Jean-Louis Chrétien, and others, are manifestly marked by Saint Augustine. Augustinian thought still resounds today in philosophical reflection. It feeds the debates about human dignity, the connections between faith and reason, or even the relation between the Earthly City and the Heavenly City.

Yes, John Paul II was right when he concluded that Augustine "has been present ever since ... in the mind and culture of the whole western world ... so that we have good reason to call him the common father of Christian Europe."[9]

[8] J.-Fr. Petit, *Saint Augustin notre contemporain: Lectures au XX^e siècle* (Paris: Bayard, 2015), 7–9.

[9] John Paul II, Apostolic Letter *Augustinum Hipponensem*, August 28, 1986; Address to the Second International Congress on Saint Augustine, September 17, 1986.

PART TWO

# SEVEN GATEWAYS
# FOR AN AUGUSTINIAN
# SPIRITUAL JOURNEY

What makes Augustine truly impressive is his "surprising modernity", as the great specialist Goulven Madec puts it. The purpose of part 2 is to show this in a general overview of his spiritual teaching.

Tackling Augustinian spirituality is like going to visit an immense "city" that has countless jewels for the sightseer. It is better to choose a few paths, to visit the most significant monuments, and to climb to the top of the church towers that dominate the skyline. By choosing seven "gateways" that open onto the spirituality of Saint Augustine, we do not claim to say everything, but simply to invite the reader to walk with him.

*Desire and Unity*: the title proposed for this book notes two major themes that help us to understand Augustine better. The preceding pages portrayed this man who was eager for happiness and truth, then starving for God. In the following chapters, "desire" will express the quest, the dynamic, the richness of being; but also the error that must be purified, the passion that needs to be evangelized, the goal that is to be determined more precisely. Augustine shows also that he thirsts for unity: personal unification, unity in friendship and charity, unity in community and in the heart of the Church.

There are good reasons why Augustine is often depicted with a flaming heart in his hand. In his quest, he never stopped loving. When he had converted, his quest led him toward the Trinity through love; he pursued it by praying and adoring. Three gateways, three initial chapters will introduce us to the theme of happiness, charity, and prayer.

A fourth chapter will lead us to the crux of our meditation: this Christ whom Augustine preached is in fact an essential figure, since he alone can reconcile the desire for God and unity in God: "Christ God is the fatherland toward which we go; Christ the man is the way by which we go."

Augustine's speculation will bring us logically to the Church and the Christian community. Through baptism and charity, we form "one man in Jesus Christ".[1] Unity is achieved in the Church, also. Conversion to life in Christ is for Augustine a conversion to the Church herself, which is "one" in Christ. Augustine invites us to be pilgrims together, in the Church, toward the Eternal City, the end of all desire.

Basically, some will say, that is nothing but Christianity.... And that would gladden the heart of Augustine, who never wanted to be idiosyncratic, but only intended to explain the pure doctrine of the Gospel.

[1] Saint Augustine, *Expositions on the Psalms*, 122, 2.

In a lecture at the Collège de France on the philosophers of antiquity, Pierre Hadot correctly emphasizes: "The work, even when it is apparently theoretical and systematic, is written not so much to inform the reader about some doctrinal content as to form him, by making him follow a certain itinerary, during which he will progress spiritually. This method is evident in the writings of Plotinus and Augustine."[2] Let us allow Augustine to guide us.

---

[2] P. Hadot, *Éloge de la philosophie antique: Leçon inaugurale de la chaire d'histoire de la pensée hellénistique et romaine faite au Collège de France, le vendredi 18 février 1983* (Paris: Allia, 1983), 49.

# CHAPTER 5

# The Quest for Happiness

While still very young, Augustine was captivated by happiness, truth, and beauty. Through the depths of his ardent soul ran an impetus that would never disappear but that was gradually converted and purified, sometimes at the cost of struggles that were painful but fruitful.

Once he had become a bishop, Augustine led his faithful to become aware of this desire for happiness, which is absolutely good in itself.[1] Every human being, he declared, carries within him an instinct for happiness, and this fundamental desire is a sort of "conspiracy of human nature", *naturae humanae conspiratio*. We all have in our hearts, as Jean Vanier put it, the "taste for happiness".[2] "It is not I alone or even a few others who wish to be happy, but absolutely everybody."[3] But where is this happiness to be found? Toward what, then, must the soul tend, with all its weight?

---

[1] For example, Saint Augustine, Sermon 306, 3–4; 150, 4; 231, 5.

[2] See his profound book: Jean Vanier, *Le Goût du bonheur* (Paris: Presses de la Renaissance, 2010).

[3] Saint Augustine, *Confessions*, X, 21, 31; cf. Saint Augustine, *On the Trinity*, XIII, 20, 25.

DEAD ENDS AND DISSATISFACTIONS

We know very well: man searches by groping, and like a moth he allows himself to be seduced by deceptive lights. He burns his wings on them. Wounded, fragile beings, we seek to possess some things that do us harm. What a tragedy these forms of false happiness are, and these dead ends where man slips and slides! "A deceitful happiness is itself a greater unhappiness."[4] On this earth, we are also malcontents, and we murmur: "When will my desire finally be sated with happiness?"[5] "Oh, if you knew what good is! The true good is not what you wish to possess; rather, what you do not consent to be—that is the good. At the word good [bonum] you sigh; at the word good you groan. Maybe even in your case sin is only an error in the choice of this good for which you are starved."[6]

Man finds that he desires without foresight a passing pleasure and that once this pleasure is experienced, he thinks about it with remorse or disgust.[7] Augustine experienced the emptiness and frustration in fleeting pleasures so much that he is, even for us, a credible witness. The bishop said, it will be necessary for "truth to set us free, so that we can be truly happy".[8] Only God will be able to offer us authentic happiness, for he alone

[4] Saint Augustine, *Expositions on the Psalms*, 129[130], 1; NPNF 1, 8:613a. Cf. Saint Augustine, *Expositions on the Psalms*, 85[86], 23: "Quia falsa felicitas, vera miseria est" (Because happiness is false, misery is true) [NPNF 1, 8:418b].

[5] Saint Augustine, *Expositions on the Psalms*, 102, 9.

[6] Saint Augustine, Sermon 72, 4; Saint Augustine, *Expositions on the Psalms*, 102, 8.

[7] Saint Augustine, Sermon 157, 5.

[8] Saint Augustine, Sermon 241, 5.

is the "supreme good" and the truth. Hence, in every human being, a background of restlessness remains. But what is it really, this restlessness?

## THE DYNAMISM OF RESTLESSNESS

August 28, 2013. On that feast of Saint Augustine, Pope Francis dedicated his homily to the kinds of "restlessness" experienced by Augustine: "The restlessness of seeking the truth, of seeking God, became the restlessness to know him ever better and of coming out of himself to make others know him. It was precisely the restlessness of love." Restlessness is, literally, an "imbalance". How suggestive Goulven Madec's translation of the opening of *The Confessions* is! "You made us to be oriented toward you; and our hearts are unbalanced [*inquietum*] as long as they have not found their equilibrium in you."[9] We all have a personal experience of this, do we not?

Yet this "imbalance" can also be considered in a very positive way. For, as Joseph Ratzinger remarked, it is the basis of "the attitude that will not let man be at peace with himself and his present state but keeps him journeying toward the eternal reality in which alone he can find repose and fulfillment."[10] Thus *The Confessions*, starting in the *cor inquietum*, the "restless heart", end

---

[9] Saint Augustine, *Confessions*, I, 1, 1. Literal English rendering of the French translation by Goulven Madec, "La conversion d'Augustin: Intériorité et communauté", *Petites études augustiniennes* (Paris: Institut des études augustiniennes, 1994), 98.

[10] Joseph Ratzinger, "Sermon for the Feast of Saint Augustine", *Dogma and Preaching*, trans. Michael J. Miller and Matthew J. O'Connell (San Francisco: Ignatius Press, 2011), 362–68 at 368.

with rest in God, in the joy of certitude: "We must ask it of you; we must seek it in you; we must knock for it at your door. Only thus shall we receive; only thus shall we find; only thus shall your door be opened. Amen."[11]

Shortly after his conversion, Augustine thought that this happiness could be reached here below. Later he would have to admit his error.[12] Only eternity will fill us completely and unify us. "How, then, do I seek you, O Lord? For when I seek you, my God, I seek a happy life. I will seek you that my soul may live. For my body lives by my soul, and my soul lives by you. How, then, do I seek a happy life . . . ? Is not the happy life the thing that all desire, and is there anyone who does not desire it at all?"[13]

## AUGUSTINIAN INTERIORITY:
## "RETURN TO YOUR HEART"

"I was far from your face in the dark shadows of passion. . . . I was thus carried toward vanity and was estranged from you, O my God."[14] The prodigal son had left for the region of "dissembling" or vanity. His return to the Father, the conversion of the sinful son, starts with a return to himself (Lk 15:17). Of course, the search for truth and happiness required Augustine first to pay attention to the external mediations (readings, meetings,

---

[11] Saint Augustine, *Confessions*, XIII, 38, 53.

[12] Saint Augustine, *Retractions*, I, 1, 2; cf. A. Solignac, *Les Confessions*, BA 14, 1996, p. 568.

[13] Saint Augustine, *Confessions*, X, 20, 29.

[14] Ibid., I, 18, 28; VII, 9, 15.

persons, etc.), which he calls *admonitiones*; but these exterior signs are preparation for interior instruction. Happiness has a fatherland, and the road passes first through our heart: "Return to your heart and from there to God, for the road from your heart to God is not long. When you are shocked by this arrangement, you have gone out of yourself, you are exiled from your own heart."[15]

Interiority is at the root of the Augustinian approach. For Augustine, the heart is the hidden place of our personal life. It is also the place of our intentions, our desires, our aspirations, and our urges.[16] The heart is the "deep self", the summit and center of our spiritual being. Augustine unceasingly invites us: "Return to your heart", *redi ad cor*.

> Lord, you heard my voice when I cried to you. This cry to God is not at all from the voice, but from the heart. Many spoke from the heart while their lips were silent, and many, too, spoke from their lips without obtaining anything, because their hearts were far away. Therefore, if you want to cry out to God, cry from the bottom of your heart, since that is where he is listening.[17]

This path is not a definitive immersion in oneself, in the mere search for a happy personal equilibrium or in a "complacent narcissism in which to contemplate one's own riches".[18] The approach presupposes going

[15] Saint Augustine, Sermon 311, 13.

[16] Cf. A. Becker, *De l'instinct du bonheur à l'extase de la béatitude* (Paris: Lethielleux, 1967), 152–54.

[17] Saint Augustine, *Expositions on the Psalms*, 30, II, 10.

[18] Jean-François Petit, *Devenir plus humain avec saint Augustin* (Paris: Salvator, 2015), 20.

out of myself toward an Other who draws me toward
him. The discovery of the Stoic and Platonic philosophers had made Augustine open to this approach of
interiority. A believer's loving faith offers him a face to
contemplate: the face of Jesus Christ:

> Where was I when I was seeking you? There you
> were, before me; but I had gone away, even from
> myself, and I could not find myself, much less you....
> He is within the inmost heart, yet the heart has wan-
> dered away from him. Return to your heart, O you
> transgressors.... You seek the blessed life in the region
> of death; it is not there.... And [Christ] departed from
> our sight that we might return to our hearts and find
> him there.[19]

## "BELIEVE IN ORDER TO UNDERSTAND"

In Augustinian spirituality, it is impossible to dissociate
the desire for happiness from the attraction of truth. The
latter was even for Augustine "the driving force of his
search".[20] Augustine the convert sang: "For a happy life
is joy in the truth. Yet this is joy in you, who are the
Truth, O God my Light."[21] The quest for happiness
and the search by the intellect will always go hand in
hand. Augustine, right after his conversion, composed
this dialogue, which sums it up well:

[19] Saint Augustine, *Confessions*, V, 2, 2; IV, 12, 18–19.
[20] Marcel Neusch, *Saint Augustin: Splendeur et misère de l'homme* (Paris: Cerf,
2011), 31.
[21] Saint Augustine, *Confessions*, X, 23, 33.

*Augustine:* I have prayed to God.
*Reason:* What then do you want to know?
*A*: All these things that I have prayed for.
*R*: Sum them up briefly.
*A*: God and the soul: that is what I desire to know.
*R*: Nothing more?
*A*: Nothing whatever.[22]

Augustine was endowed with an exceptional intellect, so that years of studying the rationalism of the Manicheans and that of the academicians or the Platonic philosophers had left him quite proud of his ability to reason. Once he had converted, would he have to renounce his intellect in his faith?

No. He was both a man of science and a man of the heart. His conversion was an experience of light that marked him forever: "light" and "illumination" are words that recur almost three thousand times in his works.[23] The result at first was bedazzlement, because God is too great for our intellect: "We speak about God; it is surprising, then, that you do not understand? If you understood, it would not be God." "Can you not understand? Believe, and you will understand."[24]

Very often Bishop Augustine comments to the faithful of his diocese on the words of Isaiah: "If you do not believe, you will not understand" (Is 7:9, Greek version). Nonetheless, in his famous Sermon 43, he affirms the harmony between the two levels, faith and reason:

---

[22] Saint Augustine, *The Soliloquies*, I, 2, 7. We will return to this expression "nothing what(so)ever".

[23] Cf. M.-A. Vannier, *Saint Augustin: La conversion en acte* (Paris: Entrelacs, 2011), 126.

[24] Saint Augustine, Sermon 117, 5, and Sermon 118; cf. Sermon 52, 16.

"Yes, it is necessary to understand in order to believe and to believe in order to understand. Do you want me to explain in a few words so that there is no more room for dispute? I will say to everyone: understand my words in order to believe, and believe the word of God in order to understand. [*Intellige, ut credas, verbum meum; crede, ut intelligas, verbum Dei.*]"[25]

These two dimensions are neither separated nor opposed; for Augustine, faith and reason are "the two forces that lead us to knowledge".[26] Although the intellect disposes us to the knowledge of God, faith is essential to it. What is at stake here proves to be quite contemporary. Thus the lecture given by Benedict XVI in Regensburg in 2006 posed this question: Are faith and reason compatible in religion, in particular in Islam? On another level, within Catholicism, some very emotional manifestations of faith sometimes seem to develop to the detriment of the intellect's activity, like two spaces hermetically sealed off from one another. All this shows the relevance of the debate.


TO KNOW IN LOVE

The truth is not just a spectacle to contemplate. Augustine desired it with every fiber of his soul. Confronted with dogma, he invites us to believe—but always in love, in the faith that acts through charity, in a living and active faith.

---

[25] Saint Augustine, Sermon 43, 9.
[26] Saint Augustine, *Against the Academicians*, III, 20, 43.

Although he speaks about the mind in search of God, Augustine associates it with the movement of the self-giving heart, supported by grace. Everywhere charity holds the reins of an intellectual life that is altogether a part of the spiritual life. An object of knowledge, truth is also an object of love, and God is truth. "We can enter into truth only through charity."[27] This makes the prayer that he addresses to God at the end of his long quest for the Trinitarian mystery shattering: "My strength and my infirmity are in your sight: preserve the one, and heal the other. My knowledge and my ignorance are in your sight; where you have opened to me, receive me as I enter."[28]

## WHEN GOD MAKES HIMSELF PRESENT TO THE HUMAN HEART

God is present in a human being; he wants to dwell there. Then the heart becomes sacred, and Augustine, with Saint Paul, develops for the faithful of his diocese the image of the temple: "Do you want to pray in a temple? Pray in yourself. But first be a temple of God, for He in His temple hears the person who prays." The soul is made to receive him: "Break those lying idols, if you want to be the temple of truth.... This day, therefore, if you promise to do so, may the Ark of the Covenant enter into your heart, and may the idols be toppled over."[29]

---

[27] Saint Augustine, *Against Faustus*, 32, 18.
[28] Saint Augustine, *On the Trinity*, XV, 28, 51 [NPNF 1, 3:227b–228a].
[29] Saint Augustine, *Homilies on the Gospel of St. John*, XV, 25 [NPNF 1, 7:106a]; Sermon 53, 7.

Augustine understood that it is "the highest Trinity which we seek when we seek God."[30] Augustine's passion for Christ, the Word of the Father, could only draw him toward the Trinity. His whole life would be a meditation on this mystery, which he would set down in writing at the conclusion of twenty years of theological labor in his treatise *On the Trinity*. He tells us that the image of God must be found in the soul of man. Thus, the soul is the image of God "in this very point, that it is capable of Him, and can be partaker of Him. Such a great good is made possible only by its being His image."[31]

In spite of our sins, despite the "dissimilarity", the image of God subsists in us, although it is "deformed". Through conversion and repentance, this image of God is renewed, and "the image begins to be reformed by the One who formed it." This is done through "daily progress as the soul is renewed" and is assimilated little by little to the image of God.[32] Grace restores the deformed image of God the Trinity in our souls, which were created so beautiful but soiled by sin.

> We also are the Image of God: not indeed that which is equal to Him [i.e., Christ, the Image of His Father], since we are made so by the Father through the Son.... We are so, because we are enlightened with light.... But we by striving imitate Him who abides, and follow Him who does not change, and by walking in Him, we reach out toward Him; because He has become for

[30] Saint Augustine, *On the Trinity*, XV, 2, 3 [NPNF 1, 3:200a].
[31] Ibid., XIV, 4, 6 [NPNF 1, 3:186a]; then XIV, 8, 11.
[32] Ibid., XIV, 15, 21; 16, 22; 17, 23.

us a way in time by His humiliation, which is to us an eternal abiding-place by His divinity.[33]

The pastor of Hippo dwells at great length on his demonstration that the human soul carries within itself the traces of the Trinity. Let us go directly to the most beautiful of his analogies, which is that of "the love, the beloved, and love". Through grace, a "trinity of love" is formed in us, a vestige of the mystery of the Father, the Son, and the Spirit of love: "Behold, then, there are three things: he that loves, and that which is loved, and love. What, then, is love, except a certain life which couples or seeks to couple together two things?"[34]

Augustine is "convinced that the Christian life is Trinitarian, or else it is not Christian".[35] And yet reason labors to understand the ineffable, inexpressible mystery; it wavers and can only remain silent. Then love introduces us to a certain knowledge of the Trinity: "The more ardently we love God, the more certainly and the more calmly we see Him."[36] The Holy Spirit, who is charity, deposits into us something like an "instructed ignorance".

Moreover, we love God and our brothers and sisters through one and the same love. For Augustine, no experience of the Trinitarian mystery is possible without the experience of fraternal charity: "You may say to me, I have not seen God; can you say to me, I have

---

[33] Ibid., VII, 3, 5 [NPNF 1, 3:108a].

[34] Ibid., VIII, 10, 14 [NPNF 1, 3:124b].

[35] A. Trapè, *Saint Augustin: L'homme, le pasteur, le mystique* (Paris: Fayard, 1988), 249.

[36] Saint Augustine, *On the Trinity*, VIII, 9, 13 [NPNF 1, 3:124b].

not seen man? Love your brother. For if you love your
brother whom you see, at the same time you shall see
God also; because you shall see Charity itself, and God
dwells within it." Thus we have the experience of the
gift, of relation, of the communion of persons, of unity:
"If you see love, you see the Trinity."[37]

Yes, "love gives us eyes to see", according to the
beautiful expression of Canon Regular Hugh of Saint
Victor. Unanimity in love becomes a path for Trinitarian contemplation.


MEDITATE WITH SAINT AUGUSTINE:
"ARDENTLY SEEK THE FACE OF GOD"

In this prayer at the end of his treatise *On the Trinity*,
Saint Augustine opens up his heart to God. And here
is this elderly scholar who reveals his soul moved by
desire, a desire that the years have not extinguished,
a desire that has found equilibrium and unification:

> Directing my purpose by this rule of faith, so far as I
>     have been able,
> so far as you have made me to be able, I have sought
>     you,
> and have desired to see with my understanding what I
>     believed;
> and I have argued and labored much.
> O Lord my God, my one hope,

[37] Saint Augustine, *Homilies on the First Epistle of St. John*, V, 7 [NPNF 1, 7:491a], and *On the Trinity*, VIII, 8, 12 [NPNF 1, 3:123a]. Cf. Soeur Marie-Ancilla, *La Règle de saint Augustin* (Paris: Cerf, 1996), 100.

hearken to me, lest through weariness I be unwilling
    to seek you,
but that I may always ardently seek your face.
Give me strength to seek,
since you made me find you, and have given the hope
    of finding you more and more.
My strength and my infirmity are in your sight:
    preserve the one, and heal the other.
My knowledge and my ignorance are in your sight;
    where you have opened to me, receive me as I
    enter;
where you have closed, open to me as I knock.
May I remember you, understand you, love you.[38]

[38] Saint Augustine, *On the Trinity*, XV, 28, 51 [NPNF 1, 3:227b–228a].

CHAPTER 6

# The Doctor of Love

## "YOUR LOVE IS YOUR WEIGHT"

Young Augustine "was in love with love".[1] After his discovery of the Ciceronian dialogue *Hortensius*, then of the academic philosophers, he loved his own research and his own thought. Once converted, he would continue to love. But what then is this force that draws our soul toward an object of desire, this force that weighs on our will so as to move it? My heaviness, my weight, is my love, Augustine says. The glutton understands this well; the lover experiences it even more passionately. A "weight" draws them on:

> The body tends toward its own place by its own gravity. A weight does not tend downward only, but moves to its own place. Fire tends upward; a stone tends downward. They are propelled by their own mass; they seek their own places. Oil poured under the water rises above the water; water poured on oil sinks under the oil. They are moved by their own mass; they seek their own places. If they are out of order, they are restless;

[1] Saint Augustine, *Confessions*, III, 1, 1.

80

when their order is restored, they are at rest. My weight is my love. By it I am carried wherever I am carried.[2]

Moreover, someone who loves identifies with what he loves, with the beloved. Having discovered that God is love, Augustine would forever remain drawn toward him. Love, elevated by grace into the love of charity, would be simultaneously the weight that drew him toward his God and the end that he desired. Because it transforms a human being in his innermost depths, charity, in short, "divinizes": it is not just a resemblance to God; it makes the soul participate in God himself, just as iron cast into the middle of the fire becomes fire through participation. "As you love, so you are! Do you love earth? You shall be earth. Do you love God? What shall I say, that you shall be a god? I dare not say it of myself; let us hear the Scriptures: 'I have said, you are gods, and all of you sons of the Most High.' "[3]

In the mystery of the covenant between God and man, charity is the element that, by divinizing, unites and embellishes the creature. "To faith, join charity. Charity is the wedding garment."[4]

This charity, a sheer gift of God, "has been poured into our hearts, not by any energies of human nature or volition, but by the Holy Spirit who is given to us, who helps our weakness and cooperates with our strength."[5] Augustine fought a lot against the Pelagians to defend

[2] Ibid., XIII, 9, 10.
[3] See Saint Augustine, *Homilies on the First Letter of St. John*, II, 14 [NPNF 1, 7:475b modified].
[4] Saint Augustine, Sermon 90, 9.
[5] Saint Augustine, *On Nature and Grace*, 70, 84 [cf. NPNF 1, 5:151b].

this absolute primacy of grace in the spiritual life. It precedes, accompanies, and follows every one of our acts.

## "LOVE AND DO WHAT YOU WILL"

Love becomes the major distinguishing mark among human beings: "Love alone makes the difference between the children of God and the children of the devil.... A mighty token, a mighty distinction! Have whatever you want; if you lack this alone, it profits you nothing. But if you lack all the rest and you have charity, you have fulfilled the Law."[6]

The way is therefore as beautiful as it is demanding! Love gives the impetus, the direction. By giving an urgent character to our acts, it confers on them their authentic perfection. Yes, the love of charity does require an "art of living"!

In this light, let us consider the famous formula: "Love and do what you will." It is not an apologia for the freedom to do anything, for license or laxism. Augustine explains it for us and, in explaining, states the requirement: "If you keep silence, keep silence for love; if you cry out, cry out for love; if you correct someone, correct him out of love; if you are sparing, be sparing out of love; let the root of love be within, and nothing can spring from this love but what is good.... Why do you fear doing evil to someone? Who does evil to the one he loves? Love; it is impossible to do this without doing good."[7]

---

[6] Saint Augustine, *Homilies on the First Epistle of St. John*, V, 7 [cf. NPNF 1, 7:490b].

[7] Ibid., VII, 8, and X, 7 [cf. NPNF 1, 7:504 and 524a].

As we see, it is not a question of doing away with morality: charity does not destroy the virtues but perfects them. It does not abolish them, it elevates them, dedicating them to the search for God. Étienne Gilson put it this way: Charity, for Augustine, is moral life itself.[8]

When charity starts, justice starts; when charity grows, justice grows; when charity is perfected, justice is perfected.[9] Fortitude is love that bears all things for what it loves. For Augustine, prudence is love that can distinguish what is useful for love and what is harmful to it. Temperance is love that gives itself totally to what it loves. Thus, "virtue is the love with which what ought to be loved is loved."[10] Delight is what love seeks. Hence the real question is no longer whether it is necessary to love, but what is necessary to love.

In matters of charity, do not stop at words, but follow through with deeds. If you are not capable of dying for your brother—that is perfect charity—"be capable of giving him some of your goods. Let charity move your heart", Augustine repeats while commenting on the First Letter of Saint John.[11] Fraternal charity becomes, so to speak, a measure of our love for God.

This love also transforms our efforts and transfigures our sacrifices: "Labor, then, will not be declined if love is present, for you know that he who loves his labor is

[8] See E. Gilson, *Introduction à l'étude de saint Augustin* (Paris: Vrin, 1949), 182–83.

[9] Saint Augustine, *On Nature and Grace*, 70, 84 [cf. n. 5]. The future distinctions made by Saint Thomas would systematize this doctrine, while preserving the motivating role of charity.

[10] Saint Augustine, Letter 167, 15 [NPNF 1, 1:537a].

[11] Saint Augustine, *Homilies on the First Epistle of St. John*, V, 12 [NPNF 1, 7:492ab].

insensible to its pain."[12] Have we not all experienced this in serving someone we love or in a work to which we are dedicated?

Between the desire for happiness and the disinterested character of charity—*agape*—there is no opposition. This charity is a gift from God that elevates and gladdens passionate love, *eros*. *Eros* and *agape* can never be completely separated from each other, Benedict XVI later wrote in his encyclical on charity.[13] For both kinds of love come from God, and human love is a "school of charity", a love that makes a person go out of himself in order to go toward the other.


## KNOWING AND LOVING ONESELF: AUGUSTINIAN OPTIMISM

The *Confessions* are not the result of merely introspective activity. Augustinian confession consists simultaneously of the acknowledgment of past sins and the praise of God's action. Through this work, Saint Augustine left in religious and literary history a uniquely subtle record of self-knowledge. It is quite foreign to "complacent narcissism"; instead, it proposes spiritual and realistic knowledge in God's sight. "Let me know you, O my Knower; let me know you even as I am known.... I would therefore confess what I know about myself; I will also confess what I do not know about myself. What I do know of myself, I know from your enlightening

[12] Saint Augustine, *Homilies on the Gospel of St. John*, XLVIII, 10, 1 [commenting on Jn 10:22, NPNF 1, 7:266a].
[13] Benedict XVI, Encyclical *God Is Love* (December 25, 2005), no. 7.

of me; and what I do not know of myself, I will continue not to know until the time when my 'darkness is as the noonday' in your sight."[14]

Confession does not cause melancholy, far from it. Instead, it contributes to the fundamental optimism of Augustinian spirituality. Benefitting from both his personal experience and his labors as a bishop, Augustine describes at great length human vices, the debasement caused by our sins. Our weaknesses are connected with original sin, which is our common frailty. We are all wounded, and psychologists repeat this rather often.

Even though we owe him the formula, Augustine did not invent the concept of original sin. Do not think that his picture of humanity is dark, because Augustine proves to be very optimistic about man, who is regenerated because of God's infinite goodness, because of Christ who is capable of re-creating us: "No man should despair of the forgiveness of his sin when those who slew Christ obtained pardon."[15]

There are [in us], as it were, two things, man and sinner. As human beings, we are God's work; the fact that we are sinners is our own doing. Blot out what you have done, so that God may save what he has done.... The very thing [sin] that displeases you would not displease you if God did not shine into you and if his truth did not show it to you.... Awake, then, while it is day; the day shines; Christ is the day.[16]

[14] Saint Augustine, *Confessions*, X, 1, 1; X, 5, 7.
[15] Saint Augustine, *Homilies on the Gospel of St. John*, XXXI, 9 [NPNF 1, 7:191b].
[16] Ibid., XII, 13–14 [NPNF 1, 7:85b–86ab].

In this light of Christ, Augustinian spirituality per-
mits a look at oneself that is both realistic and positive; it leads to a true love of self. "He, therefore, who
knows how to love himself, loves God."[17] Augustine
invites us to take an initial step: mercy toward ourselves. We must love ourselves; otherwise, we run the
risk of not loving God the Creator who gave us being.
"What does it mean to give alms? It is to perform an act
of mercy. And what does it mean to perform an act of
mercy? If you are well-advised, start with yourself....
Return to your conscience; there you will find a soul
begging, a soul that is in need, in poverty.... Therefore if you have faith, you must show it by feeding your
soul first."[18]

## LOVING ALL THINGS IN GOOD: *UTI ET FRUI*

When he converted, did Augustine have to give up
happiness? Did he have to renounce desire, the attraction of enjoying the good things in life? Let us listen to
him instead:

> Who can live without affection? And do you suppose,
> brethren, that those who fear God, worship God, love
> God, have no affections?... The drunkard rejoices, and
> should the just man not rejoice? The former is unfortu-
> nate, even if he gets drunk; blessed is the latter, even if
> he is hungry and thirsty.... Let him see the suffering of
> the former and his own joy, and let him think of God.

[17] Saint Augustine, *On the Trinity*, XIV, 14, 18 [NPNF 1, 3:192b].
[18] Saint Augustine, Sermon 106, 3.

He who now gives us such joy in our faith, in hope, in charity, in the truth of the Scriptures, what is he not preparing for the end?![19]

Saint Augustine describes a "delectable sense" as a deep but highly purified spiritual reality. "There is a delight in the Lord", which is capable of delighting us even more than the things that he created.[20] "But what is it that I love in loving you?... I love a certain kind of light and sound and fragrance and food and embrace in loving my God, who is the light and sound and fragrance and food and embracement of my inner man.... This is what I love when I love my God."[21]

Augustine also continues to be the man of wonder who sings the beauty of the creatures and the splendors of the world. Things can participate in their Creator by receiving from him a certain trace or resemblance: "You, O Lord,... created these things. You are beautiful; thus they are beautiful. You are good, thus they are good. You are; thus they are. But they are not as beautiful, nor as good, nor as truly real as you their Creator are."[22]

Augustine sees in the sprouting of a seed a prodigious work of his God. As a precursor of Christian ecology, he leads us to admire the natural order, in which God stands at the center: "I admire all this, I sing of it, but I still thirst for the one who made all this."[23] Through creation, he was able to bless and seek his Creator.

[19] Saint Augustine, *Expositions on the Psalms*, 77, 13 [NPNF 1, 8:364a], and 58, 22.
[20] Ibid., 32, II, 6.
[21] Saint Augustine, *Confessions*, X, 6, 8.
[22] Ibid., XI, 4, 6.
[23] Saint Augustine, *Expositions on the Psalms*, 41, 7.

A distinction familiar to Augustine will shed light on this spirituality of the "temporal order": "Use [*uti*] well the things here below, and you will correctly enjoy [*frui*] the good from above."[24] Someone who is engaged in earthly realities should make good, orderly, and moderate use of the things of this world, of relative goods (money, power, possessions, etc.). This binomial *uti/frui*—for using things as a means—is a foundation of Augustinian ethics. "These inferior values have their delights",[25] but as means in the *ordo amoris*, in the order of love that always tends toward God. "We too make use of them, but for the needs of our pilgrimage, without making our happiness depend on them, because we could be carried away with them. Indeed, we make use of this world as though we were not using it (1 Cor 7:31), and it is with the intention of reaching the One who made the world, to dwell in him and to enjoy his eternity with him."[26]

Could it be that Augustine, like other Fathers of the Church, devalued sexuality? Some have claimed it. Certainly Augustine speaks to us as a convert; he had loved very badly, and therefore he wanted to exorcise the tortuous paths of the sinner. To arrive at happiness, sensuality and ambition are not the right shortcuts. Book X of the *Confessions* reveals this reserve of a man who for too long had gone astray in sensuality. Nevertheless, Augustine's moral virtue has nothing of that "Puritan repression that casts a troubled

---

[24] Saint Augustine, Sermon 21, 3.
[25] Saint Augustine, *Confessions*, II, 5, 10.
[26] Saint Augustine, Sermon 157, 5.

glance at the things beyond the barrier that is not crossed."[27]

Ultimately, we will be able to rest and enjoy—*frui*—eternally in God alone. All other things are to be used: *uti*. Since an instrument is made to be played, let us not break it! And so, "do not condemn the flesh; only destroy sin so as to make nature live."[28] When he speaks about gifts received from God, Augustine gives thanks. He dares to ask that, purified, these gifts might be preserved for him and even developed![29]

Here we have one feature of Augustinian asceticism: giving the right pitch, tuning the life of our senses to the search for God. Although the French poet Mallarmé writes, "The flesh is sad", Augustine, in contrast, dares to sing about the joy of the transfigured body, which is capable of being something other than an instrument of sadness and sin.

> In order to serve as a model for you, he took in you the means by which to die for you. He took in you the means by which to offer sacrifice for you, so as to instruct you by his example. What did he have to teach you? That you are to rise again.... We are risen because Christ is risen; because it was by no means the Word who died and then rose again; but it was the flesh that, in the Word, died and then rose again. Christ died in this flesh that must die in you, and rose in this same flesh in which you are to rise again.[30]

[27] H.-I. Marrou, *Saint Augustin et l'augustinisme* (Paris: Seuil, 2003), 64.
[28] Saint Augustine, Sermon 184, 2.
[29] Saint Augustine, *Confessions*, I, 19, 31.
[30] Saint Augustine, *Expositions on the Psalms*, LXXI, 10.

EXPANDING DESIRE

Augustine leads us by the road of charity toward our heavenly homeland. Benedict XVI explains that Augustine "thought he had found the Truth in prestige, in his career, in the possession of things ...; he committed faults, he experienced sorrows, he faced failures, but he never stopped."[31] As a convert, Augustine was still a soul filled with desire:

> Let us then seek in order to find him; let us seek him even after having found him. In order to find him, it is necessary to seek him, for he is hidden; even after finding him, we must seek him again, for he is immense. Hence another passage says, "Seek His face always." For he satisfies the seeker to the utmost of his capacity; and makes the finder still more capable, that he may seek to be filled anew, according to the growth of his ability to receive.[32]

Augustine's teaching is eloquent: God puts off giving himself to me and, thus, expands my desires; by expanding them, he enlarges my heart; in enlarging it, he makes me more and more able to receive him. "Let us desire therefore, my brethren, for we shall be filled."[33] Augustine is truly a teacher of the desire for God. Our life is dynamism, desire, and tension of love; the desire to know, to love, and to be loved. Our

[31] Benedict XVI, General Audience, August 25, 2010.
[32] Saint Augustine, *Homilies on the Gospel of St. John*, LXIII, 1 [cf. NPNF 1, 7:314ab].
[33] Saint Augustine, *Homilies on the First Epistle of St. John*, IV, 6 [NPNF 1, 7:485a].

whole spiritual life therefore contains the capacity to
make progress:

> Advance, my brethren; examine yourselves constantly
> without deceiving or flattering or coddling your-
> selves.... If you ever say, "That is enough!" then you
> perish. Keep adding, keep walking, keep making prog-
> ress! Do not stop along the way, do not go back, do not
> go astray. The one who does not make progress remains
> immobile; the one who turns again to the place he set
> out from goes backward; the one who loses the faith
> loses his way.

Although he is demanding, Augustine remains realistic. The pastor will not object if he sees us hesitat-
ing, falling, or limping. A true father who understands
our weaknesses, he continues his preaching: "Not to
advance is to stop; to turn back is to fall again into the
disorders that you have given up. To stray is to wander
from the path. It is better to walk on the road limping
than to be running somewhere off the path."[34]

But what sort of progress are we talking about? For
Augustine, holiness lies principally in the progress of
charity. Asceticism that mortifies the body is not characteristic of the spirituality that he proposes, whereas it
was widespread among the Desert Fathers. The heart of
Augustinian asceticism lies in the battle against all the
egotisms of the self that paralyze progress in love. Asceticism has no value in itself, but it places itself at the service of progress in the virtues, particularly in charity.[35]

[34] Saint Augustine, Sermon 169, 18.

[35] See Soeur Marie-Ancilla, *La Charité et l'Unité: clé pour entrer dans la théologie
de saint Augustin* (Paris: Mame, "Cahiers de l'École Cathédrale", 1993), 67.

Charity never reaches the end of its desires. Through it, we will hunger for God and always thirst for his presence.[36] We are going to God, from one ascent to the next. These ascents (which are found in our hearts) are paced especially by the Beatitudes taught by Jesus in his Sermon on the Mount. Augustine sees that this discourse of Christ is "a perfect standard of the Christian life" with "all the precepts by which the Christian life is moulded."[37] The Beatitudes start in poverty—"Blessed are the poor"—which for Augustine is a fundamental humility. This path of our progress ascends toward wisdom, that is, contemplation of the truth, which gives peace to the whole man and makes him like God.

Our charity has therefore expanded. But to what point can it grow? "The measure of the love of God is to love without measure." We know that this formula, so dear to Saint Bernard, is also by Augustine himself.[38] Little by little, this gift will be measured against the Giver, the Triune God.


## MEDITATE WITH SAINT AUGUSTINE: THE JOY OF LOVING

In this passage, Saint Augustine shows that the Christian does not have to abandon his desire for joy and his love for beauty. In God he finds all this:

---

[36] Saint Augustine, Sermon 53, 11.

[37] Saint Augustine, *On the Sermon on the Mount*, I, 1 [NPNF 1, 6:3a].

[38] Saint Augustine, Sermon Dolbeau, 11, 9. In letter 119, Severus replies to his friend Augustine, certainly quoting him. Cf. S. Lancel, *Saint Augustin* (Paris: Fayard, 1999), 283.

But what is it that I love in loving you?

Not physical beauty, nor the splendor of time,
nor the radiance of the light—so pleasant to our
    eyes—
nor the sweet melodies of the various kinds of songs,
nor the fragrant smell of flowers and ointments and
    spices;
not manna and honey,
not the limbs embraced in physical love—
it is not these I love when I love my God.
Yet it is true that I love a certain kind of light and
    sound and fragrance and food and embrace in
    loving my God,
who is the light and sound and fragrance and food and
    embracement of my inner man—
where that light shines into my soul which no place
    can contain,
where time does not snatch away the lovely sound,
where no breeze disperses the sweet fragrance,
where no eating diminishes the food there provided,
and where there is an embrace that no satiety comes to
    sunder.
This is what I love when I love my God.[39]

[39] Saint Augustine, *Confessions*, X, 6, 8.

## Chapter 7

# "Your Desire Is Your Prayer"

### PRAYER, SURGE OF THE HEART

Even in prayer, Augustine remains the man of desire.
For him, the desire of God, sustained by love, will blossom in acts of prayer. To pray is to express all the deep
surges of our heart: "Desire is a continual prayer, even
when the tongue remains silent. If you do not stop
desiring, you do not stop praying. When does prayer
sleep? When desire has grown cold."[1]

This certainly is a reassuring view, but it is equally
demanding: someone can pray without having to con-
struct or verbalize it or even be aware of it. Prayer is
already present where nothing remains but the poor
spark of a mute desire, in its minimum of love. The
demanding aspect of prayer lies precisely in love. And
so Augustine warns us:

> In the soul there is an incessant prayer, which is desire.
> Whatever you do, you do not cease at all to pray if
> you desire the rest of heaven. Therefore, if you do not
> want to interrupt your prayer, do not interrupt your

[1] Saint Augustine, Sermon 80, 7.

desire. An incessant desire is a continual voice. To be
silent would be to love no more. Who, then, fell silent?
Those about whom it says: "And because wickedness
is multiplied, most men's love will grow cold" (Mt
24:12). The chilling of charity is the silence of the heart;
the flame of charity, on the contrary, is the cry of the
heart. If charity remains fervent, you always cry out; if
you always cry out, you always desire.[2]

"Why does God, who knows everything, ask us to
pray?" Who has not asked himself this question at one
time or another? Augustine answers Proba, a Roman
widow: Prayer is not necessary for God, because he is
not unaware of any of our desires, but it is necessary for
man. It helps to deepen our desire, to broaden it, so as
to conform it little by little to God's will for us. Thus
prayer makes us capable of receiving the gift that he is
preparing for us.[3]

Augustine advises Proba to simplify her way of praying, because prayer makes progress especially in love.
But how? Quite simply through our groans, our inartic-
ulate words, or even our tears, which Augustine often
considers to be signs of intense prayer. What purpose do
words serve, then, in prayer? Their role is pedagogical,
so that we might be attentive to what we are asking,
but "not to instruct God about our needs or to bend his
will".[4] In a way, prayer interrogates me, it calls my certitudes into question. This is why the Lord asks us to pray
much, to "knock on God's door" tirelessly. By opening

[2] Saint Augustine, *Expositions on the Psalms*, 37, 14.
[3] See Saint Augustine, *Letter to Proba*, 17.
[4] Ibid., 19–21.

me up to the discovery of this will of God, prayer
makes me enter into his mystery of mercy. "The praises
that we offer to God do not increase him, but rather
us; your praises do not lift up the Lord at all.... God
who gives us these lessons is essentially unchangeable;
how much less, then, will he himself be made greater
by your praises, or diminished by your insults! But since
we stand to benefit from praising the Lord, he orders us
to do so as a result of his mercies, not of his demands."[5]

Let us remember well that last sentence. Before considering the duty to pray, let us look at the requirement
of prayer as a mercy from God. That certainly turns our
perspective upside down! How many times have we
put the emphasis on the duty? This is quite real but
secondary, and it is nourished by love. We enter into
God's wisdom through prayer; we perceive better what
he wants of us; we expand our hearts in expectation. By
adjusting our will to God's, we enter into the perspective of happiness that is prepared in his fatherly heart,
which he wants to offer to us.


"ASK GOD FOR GOD ALONE"


Prayer is therefore a mystery of reception, preparation
for God's gifts. But what gifts should we ask for? There
are, quite obviously, some legitimate earthly requests,
those pertaining to life, health, the goods of the heart.
As we do, the faithful of the bishop's diocese often asked
for excessively material goods. Augustine often reminded

---

[5] Saint Augustine, *Expositions on the Psalms*, 134, 1.

them to pray also in order to obtain the virtues of courage, fortitude, chastity, or justice. But beyond the gifts of God, it is necessary to ask for God himself. "You have desired so much from him; I beg you, desire that he give you the gift of himself. In these goods there are no more delights than in himself, and there is no way that anyone could compare them with him. Therefore, the one who prefers God himself, from whom he has received all these goods, to these same gifts that are his joy, calls on God in truth."[6]

Augustine always ends by concluding: in your place, I would not stop there. By centering the faithful on God again, he finally teaches them to ask God only for God himself. He teaches this lesson by having the Lord say: "I am the one that you must possess; I must be your delight." The bishop finishes his homily with a prayer pronounced aloud: "I will not be satisfied with perishable goods; I will not be satisfied with temporal goods. May the Lord give me something eternal; may he give me his own wisdom; may he give me his Word, God in God, may he give me himself, God the Father, Son, and Holy Spirit. I stand like a beggar at his door."[7]

We keep coming back to this. What we should ask God for is God: "Call on God for God", and not for perishable goods. "Love God for God's sake", and "do not ask God to become the assistant of your greed"!

Augustine saw the Lord's Prayer as the prayer of petition par excellence. This is because the Master is the one who taught it to us. It is because the seven petitions that it contains sum up and collect all the requests that we can make. Augustine never stops exhorting us: "You are not to ask for things besides what is expressed in this prayer."[8] The Our Father speaks about God and about ourselves, about his kingdom and the way in which we can get to it; it mentions our needs, the difficult task of forgiveness, the devil and temptations. This prayer misses nothing, and "if we pray with words that come from ourselves, we must conform them to the spirit of this prayer." Augustine brings us to the heart of Christian prayer, offering to purify our ways of doing it: "It is necessary to pray, it is necessary to pray sincerely, it is necessary to pray as the Master taught us to."[9] His word has not grown old.

Distractions and dryness in prayer are inevitable. Who has not experienced it? In some sermons, Augustine does seem to be speaking about himself, a bishop overwhelmed with responsibilities. Here in one passage he mentions a man who prays, whose "thoughts flutter from these desires to others", with his soul torn between cares and distractions. He has to accept this humiliating, almost inevitable imperfection. When he questions his soul about the authenticity of his prayer, it answers him: "I do it as much as I can, but weakly, languidly, inconstantly."[10] Here again, Augustine proves to be very human.

All things considered, he speaks about us; he speaks for us. As a true father and pastor, Augustine encourages us above all to persevere in prayer. Until the evening of his life, until his final breath, he gave witness to this

[8] Saint Augustine, Sermon 56, 4.
[9] Saint Augustine, *Expositions on the Psalms*, 103, I, 19.
[10] Ibid., 145, 6.

perseverance. He was a man of prayer because he was a man who desired God.


THANKSGIVING AND PRAISE

A Christian, unlike a pagan, does not seek to show his God. His is invisible. But creation, in its perceptible beauty, can lead man's meditation toward the Creator himself. Augustine sees in this a necessary stage of the spiritual life: we must ascend toward God through material, visible things. This pathway passes through our hearts, because this is the sanctuary where the "alchemy" that separates good from evil is at work, purifying and putting in order the love of created things.

Augustine then offers us a very beautiful approach. Indeed, creatures, by themselves, have neither voices nor hearts with which to praise God. And yet: "They themselves praise God in a way.... How do they praise the Lord? It is because when we see them, we call to mind the supreme craftsman who created them, and from this comes the praise of God in us; now, when we praise God by considering all creatures, all creatures praise God."[11]

The Christian becomes, so to speak, the "priest of creation"; he is the mediator who offers it to God. The soul dedicated to praise—"the eucharistic soul"—makes earth the pathway to heaven.

Yes, Augustine invites us to become men and women of thanksgiving, witnesses to praise. Note well: not only

---

[11] Ibid., 148, 3.

when we have an abundance, are healthy, or enjoy
success. . . .

> No, rather at all times; in other words, both in this
> moment and also when this prosperity is clouded,
> whether for a time or by order of the Lord, when these
> goods will be taken from you, when they develop
> more sparsely, when they disappear as soon as they
> have developed. . . . He is the one who gives them, he is
> the one who takes them away; but he never withdraws
> from the one who blesses him.[12]

We have not forgotten the context of Augustine's
life: uncertainty about the future, social injustices. And
here the bishop invites his flock to give thanks! What
a demand for us, who often respond to God's benev-
olence with a pessimistic view, seeing only the "half-
empty glass". Augustine invites us to acquire a very
profound disposition: let us glorify God, not by bringing
him something that was ours, but by giving back and
offering to him his own gifts. For everything has come
to us through him.

Joy and thanksgiving correspond to the most authentic posture of a Christian who allows God himself to
act in his heart through his gifts. In this Augustinian
optimism, the human being who lived totally in thanksgiving would be a "Christified" Christian, incorporated
into his Savior: "Is there anything better for us to have
in our heart or utter with our lips or record with our
pen than this? Thanks be to God! No other phrase is
more easily spoken, and nothing more pleasant in sound,
profound in significance, and profitable in practice than

---

[12] Ibid., 33, II, 3–4.

this: *Deo gratias!*"[13] In the next world, our praise will be eternal and uninterrupted, and our desires will be fulfilled by God himself.

## MEDITATE WITH SAINT AUGUSTINE: "SING BY YOUR ACTIONS"

Saint Augustine demands consistency of us. The truth of prayer is proved above all in the commitment of a life. Prayer is also a sign, which must not lie; it must reflect the profound authenticity of our interior charity, and it commits us to unity of life:

> Praise the Lord ... but praise with your whole selves: that is, let not your tongue and voice alone praise God, but your conscience also, your life, your deeds. For now, when we are gathered together in the Church, we praise: when we go forth each to his own business, we seem to cease to praise God. Let a man not cease to live well, and then he always praises God. To stop praising God is to stray from justice and from all that pleases him. If you never separate yourself from the good, your tongue may very well fall silent, but your life is a song, and God has his ear on your heart.... Now, God willed to leave it to your choice, whom you want to prepare a place for in your heart, for God or for the devil. When you have prepared it, the one who possesses your heart will command in that place. Therefore, my brethren, do not stop at the sound alone; when you praise God, praise him fully. Sing with your voice, sing by a holy life, sing by your actions.[14]

[13] Saint Augustine, Letter 41, 1 [NPNF 1, 1:275a].
[14] Saint Augustine, *Expositions on the Psalms*, 148, 2 [NPNF 1, 8:673b].

# CHAPTER 8

# Christ, "Way and Fatherland"

## THE EXPERIENCE OF CHRIST THE SAVIOR

Jesus Christ is unceasingly present on Augustine's lips. Is this because the bishop had to defend Christ, true God and true man, in incessant battles against heresies? Not only and not chiefly for that reason. For Augustine, to convert was to encounter God made man and to be incorporated into him. The bishop of Hippo does not propose in the first place a teaching but, rather, an experience of spiritual life in Christ Jesus: "Christ was decisive in his life, and it was precisely by staking his life on him that Augustine had access to his mystery."[1]

We seek happiness and truth; we are souls imbued with the desire for God. But we cannot see God, and yet it was necessary to seek him. And so God became man, so that we could see him; and in seeing him, walk after him: "that there might be a way for man to man's God through the God-man."[2] Since he is entirely on

[1] J. Doré, "Présentation", in Goulven Madec, *La Patrie et la Voie: Le Christ dans la vie et la pensée de saint Augustin* (Paris: Desclée, 1989), 9.

[2] Saint Augustine, *The City of God*, XI, 2 [NPNF 1, 2:206a]. Compare the overview by Marcel Neusch, *Saint Augustin: L'amour sans mesure* (Paris: Parole et Silence, 2001), 113–36.

God's side, and entirely on our side, Christ is the perfect mediator; he saves us and opens up for us the way to the Father: "Christ is the gate. This gate was opened when his side was pierced by the lance. Remember what flowed from it, and look at how you will be able to enter. When he was hanging on the Cross dying, the Lord had his side opened with a lance, and from it gushed water and blood: one purifies you; the other serves as your ransom."[3]

Is this an "ethereal", idealized Christ that Bishop Augustine proposes? No. We have seen Augustine describe Jesus' weariness or his tactful compassion toward the adulterous woman. "Christ took without sin the whole human nature, in order that he might heal the whole man from the plague of sin."[4] This union of the two natures in Jesus Christ is beautiful; it is even the principle of beauty for Augustine the humanist, influenced by the esthetic of antiquity. For him, Christ is beauty: "He alone is the fairest one, who loved the foul to make them fair."[5] Augustine's delicate soul is revealed when he sings the harmony of the apparent paradoxes.

May the Bridegroom always appear in his beauty for us who believe. He is beautiful as God, since the Word is God; he is beautiful in the Virgin's womb, where he clothes himself in human nature without divesting himself of divine nature; he is beautiful in his birth, this infant Word.... He is therefore beautiful in heaven

[3] Saint Augustine, Sermon 311, 3.
[4] Saint Augustine, *The City of God*, X, 27 [NPNF 1, 2:197b].
[5] Saint Augustine, *Homilies on the Gospel of St. John*, X, 13 [cf. NPNF 1, 7:74b].

and beautiful on earth, beautiful in the Virgin's womb, beautiful in his mother's arms, beautiful in his miracles and beautiful in his scourging, beautiful when he invites us into his life, beautiful when he scorns death, beautiful when he lays down his life and beautiful when he takes it up again, beautiful on the cross, beautiful in the tomb, beautiful in heaven.[6]

Augustine forms our viewpoint as Christians. He invites us to recognize a beauty becoming incarnate in poverty, the littleness of children, or the slow gestures of an elderly person, just as much as in the most complete or the most transfigured forms.

The bishop of Hippo is eloquent when he describes "the admirable commerce" through which the incarnate Word comes to save us, when he speaks about this strange and "divine merchant"! His words must have touched his contemporaries in that port city of sailors and shopkeepers. He wants them to become vibrant through their own encounter with Christ, knowing all too well what he himself exchanged with his Savior in the dazzling shock of his conversion. With his God, he bartered misery and sin for the life of God himself:

This divine merchant [*mercator*] brought us invaluable goods from his country, while in ours he found only what you meet with everywhere. What is there an abundance of here?... Birth and death, those are the things that earth is full of; and so the Savior was born so as then to die.... He took death and stifled it, as a powerful gladiator takes hold of a lion until it stops breathing. In him there was no principle of death, nor any

---

[6] Saint Augustine, *Expositions on the Psalms*, 44, 3.

principle of life in us; therefore, he took the death that comes from us in order to give us the life that comes from him.[7]

From now on, happiness has a destination and a pathway: Christ our God "is the fatherland toward which we go, [as man] he is the way by which we go. Let us go to him through him, and we will not get lost."[8]

## CHRIST OUR "SACRAMENT"

For Augustine, Christ is at the same time example and *sacramentum*, "sacrament". We easily understand that Jesus Christ is exemplary. But what does "sacrament" mean for this theologian, as for so many Fathers of the Church? It is not exactly what we understand the term to mean today, but a broader and very profound idea. Thus, Christ's Resurrection offers the example of what we will be, and it becomes the *sacramentum* that gives life to the soul. A source of grace, the *sacramentum* is at the same time a sign and a cause of salvation. From this perspective, the corporeal humanity of Jesus is presented as a medicinal remedy that is at the same time a visible example and a "sacrament" for the believer. By touching in this way Christ Jesus, who joins us today, we insert our "self" into his.[9]

---

[7] Saint Augustine, Sermon 233, 4, and 232, 5.

[8] Saint Augustine, Sermon 92, 3.

[9] Saint Augustine, *On the Trinity*, IV, 3, 6. Cf. *Homilies on the Gospel of St. John*, XXXV, 6. Compare Joseph Ratzinger (Benedict XVI), *Jesus of Nazareth: Holy Week: From the Entrance into Jerusalem to the Resurrection*, trans. the Vatican Secretariat of State (San Francisco: Ignatius Press, 2011), 274.

Paganism exalted the power of Aesculapius, the "divine physician". Like other Fathers of the Church, Augustine describes Christ as the true and divine physician. Today, medical science could very well be this new, super-powerful Aesculapius, for the modern man focused on his bodily health. Augustine remains relevant when he recalls that the same word *salus* in Latin means "salvation" and "health".[10] For him, to save is also to heal! Christ is the physician par excellence, who alone can heal me in my inmost depths: Augustine confides to the Lord, "Tu, medice meus intime" [my most secret physician], which could be translated: "O you, physician of my deepest being".[11] With the convert Augustine, let us allow God to heal us "in our inmost depths" through the sufferings of his humanity: "By His very nativity [the Word] made an eye-salve to cleanse the eyes of the heart and to enable us to see His majesty by means of His humility.... He healed our eyes; and what follows? 'And we beheld His glory' (Jn 1:14). His glory no one can see unless healed by the humility of His flesh.... That Physician made for you an eye-salve."[12]

Thus, the humility of Christ enters into the process of our healing as a mysterious remedy, "the foremost remedy [*medicamentum*] by which the swelling of our pride may be cured and the profound mystery [*sacramentum*] by which the bond of sin may be loosed."[13]

---

[10] Cf. H. Vermès, "La *salus* dans la règle de saint Augustin: une préoccupation de la santé ou du salut?", in Jean-François Petit, O. Roduit. eds., *Actualité de la spiritualité augustinienne* (Paris: Salvator, 2018), 69–91.

[11] Saint Augustine, *Confessions*, X, 3, 4 [NPNF 1, 1:143a].

[12] Saint Augustine, *Homilies on the Gospel of St. John*, II, 16 [NPNF 1, 7:18b].

[13] Saint Augustine, *On the Trinity*, VIII, 5, 7 [NPNF 1, 3:119a].

With a certain audacity, Augustine can say that God became humble, as he says that God became man: "The Son of God came down to earth and humbled himself. O man, why do you pride yourself? Because of you, God humbled himself. It would repel you, no doubt, to follow a man in the path of humility; then at least imitate the humility of a God." Without in any way giving up magnanimity or heroism, humility will become the path to working for true greatness.

Perhaps you expected to hear Divine Wisdom say: Learn from me how I formed the heavens and the stars. . . . You were wrong; first she will say: Learn that I am meek and humble of heart. Consider, my brethren, what you have to learn first; surely it is a little thing. We aspire to what is great; in order to become great, let us become attached to what is little. Would you like to deal with God's greatness? Deal first with his humility.[14]

The more Augustine advanced in age and experience, the more he highlighted this decisive role of humility in the dynamism toward holiness. "There is nothing more excellent than the way of charity, but only the humble are able to walk on it."[15] Humility is, properly speaking, a fundamental virtue, because it makes us truthful in God's sight, beggars seeking faith and his love. It becomes a way of truth for man: because "Your whole humility is to know yourself."[16] Humility

[14] Saint Augustine, Sermon 117, 17.
[15] Saint Augustine, *Expositions on the Psalms*, 141, 7.
[16] Saint Augustine, *Homilies on the Gospel of St. John*, XXV, 16 [NPNF 1, 7:166a].

is furthermore a "primordial" virtue because it disposes us to receive all the other virtues.

## CHRIST, OUR FRIEND AND INTERIOR TEACHER

Through faith, hope, and charity, I truly participate in the mystery of Christ. "Participation", a key idea in Augustinian spirituality, means much more than "to take part" in the life and the grace of Christ. It refers to a very deep—we might say ontological—relation between the person and his Creator.[17] The path that opens up will be the path of happiness and spiritual enjoyment. To follow Christ is "to enjoy the truth, to enjoy justice, to enjoy eternal life, for Christ is all this." Through grace, a solidarity that is initiated at baptism binds me to Christ, just as the solidarity of wounded human nature associates me with Adam.[18] Jesus Christ is that much more ours in our hearts because he incorporates us into himself. The enthusiastic, very Pauline expressions of Augustine must become ours: "Let us give thanks that we are made not only Christians, but Christ. Do you understand, brethren, the grace of God that God bestowed on us in giving us Christ as our Head? Marvel and rejoice, for we have become Christ."[19]

The spiritual man is truly Christ in us, as Joseph Ratzinger put it: "Certainly, the concept of the *homo*

---

[17] Cf. P. Sambor, *La Participation sacramentelle: Une entrée dans la dynamique de la vie divine d'après les sermons au peuple de saint Augustin* (Münster: Aschendorff, 2017), 17–19.

[18] Saint Augustine, *Homilies on the Gospel of St. John*, XXVI, 4; Saint Augustine, *Expositions on the Psalms*, 95, 15.

[19] Ibid., XXI, 8 [cf. NPNF 1, 7:140b].

*interior* is an exclusively salvific concept, but this *homo interior* is not a hidden sphere within the limits of the self; the true *homo interior* for us all is Christ, Christ incarnate, with his human body."[20] Christ achieves unity among us. Even though he has ascended into heaven, Christ is still our teacher and spiritual master; "he departed from our sight that we might return to our hearts and find him there."[21] Expanded by love, faith opens the way to union: "What does it mean, then, to believe in him? It means to combine love with faith, to love him by believing, to go to him through faith and to be incorporated with his members."[22]

Thus we commune with Christ, grafted on the One who is the Vine.

Within us, Christ watches and teaches. Then let us return to our hearts! In a meditation on the storm that Jesus calmed, Augustine describes him asleep in the boat, on the Lake of Tiberias, which is stirred up by the storm. My life is a boat, my heart is troubled and agitated, but Christ seems to be sleeping. This apparent sleep of Jesus is the "sleep" of my faith. Then the bishop calls out to me: "Therefore awaken Christ! Awaken your faith! Picture that future life with the eyes of faith."[23] You will find peace and strength.

Paul VI declared that Saint Augustine, "more than anyone, spoke about the interior teacher",[24] the one

---

[20] Joseph Ratzinger, *Peuple et maison de Dieu dans l'ecclésiologie de saint Augustin* (Perpignan-Paris: Artège-Lethielleux, 2017), 324.

[21] Saint Augustine, *Confessions*, IV, 12, 19.

[22] Saint Augustine, *Homilies on the Gospel of St. John*, XXIX, 6 [*sic*]; cf. XXVII, 7.

[23] Saint Augustine, *Expositions on the Psalms*, 147, 3.

[24] Paul VI, Allocution, December 30, 1970.

who speaks in the heart itself. The bishop of Hippo is quite convinced of the role that has been allotted to him. As the action of the tree grower is performed on the exterior of the tree, that of the preacher is performed on the exterior of souls. Thus, it prepares for the action of the interior teacher, which is performed in the depths of the heart. Preachers, counselors, and spiritual directors must make this teaching their own; it is the prerequisite for the self-effacement necessary in the presence of God's work: "Take it as certain that, even if you might learn something good from me, your true teacher will always be the interior teacher whom you will hear in your soul; he is the one who will make you recognize the truth of what I have told you; for the one who plants is nothing, nor the one who waters, but everything comes from God, who gives the growth."[25]

The word of God, ceaselessly preached and commented on by the bishop, is a privileged mediation. Had Augustine not experienced its effective power in the garden in Milan? It offers, so to speak, a *sacramentum* of Christ. For Augustine, the Scriptures are "very fertile pastures" to feed us and heal us, because as a whole the Bible "relates Christ and places the emphasis on charity".[26] The Old Testament itself prepared in a veiled manner for Christ, the one who was to reveal himself in the New, thus revealing his saving love. "Therefore, if you lack the time to pore over all the sacred pages [of the Bible], to unroll all the scrolls of their speeches, to delve into all the secrets of the Scriptures, take charity,

[25] Saint Augustine, Letter 266, 4; *Homilies on the Gospel of St. John*, III, 15.
[26] Saint Augustine, Sermon 46, 24; Saint Augustine, *Catechism of the Uninstructed*, 4, 8; and Letter 21, 3.

in which everything is summed up.... What you understand in the Scriptures is charity uncovered; what you do not understand is charity under cover."[27]

## MARY, MOTHER OF THE INCARNATE WORD

"One cannot think of the reality of the Incarnation without referring to Mary, the Mother of the Incarnate Word."[28] These words of Saint John Paul II could have been penned by Augustine, for it was part of the logic of his conversion to the incarnate God, who became a humble child in Mary. In exhorting his faithful to prepare for Christmas, he ceaselessly refers to the Mother of God. Mary's title, "Virgin", is dear to him, as a proof of God's almighty power. Augustine deeply perceives how spiritual this mystery of Mary's "yes" was: the sign of a childbirth by the heart through faith, which she offered as a model:

> Mary is more blessed in receiving the faith of Christ than in conceiving the flesh of Christ. For to someone who said, "Blessed is the womb which bore you", he himself replied, "Rather, blessed are they who hear the word of God, and keep it." Lastly, to his brethren, that is, his kindred according to the flesh, who did not believe in him, what profit was there in being his relatives? Thus also her nearness as a mother would have done Mary no good had she not borne Christ in her heart in a more blessed manner than in her flesh.[29]

[27] Saint Augustine, Sermon 350, 2.

[28] John Paul II, Encyclical Redemptoris Mater, On the Blessed Virgin Mary in the Life of the Pilgrim Church (March 25, 1987), no. 5.

[29] Saint Augustine, Holy Virginity, 3 [NPNF 1, 3:418a].

Along this Marian line, Augustine invites us to interiorize our faith in the mystery of Christ: "What you admire externally in Mary, reproduce in the interior of your soul. To believe in your heart in order to be justified is to conceive Christ; to confess with your lips in order to be saved is to give birth to him."[30]

I bear Christ in my life; he dwells in my heart, and I can offer him to my brethren.


BECOMING A SOURCE OF MERCY

Augustine recalls that, being grafted onto Jesus Christ, I possess in my heart this mercy offered by God.[31] After all, the Gospel of John records Christ's promise: "Jesus stood up and proclaimed, 'If any one thirst, let him come to me and drink. He who believes in me, as the Scripture has said, 'Out of his heart shall flow rivers of living water' (Jn 7:37–38)." Augustine enthusiastically comments:

> The Lord, therefore, cries aloud to us to come and drink, if we thirst within; and He says that when we have drunk, rivers of living water shall flow from our belly. The belly of the inner man is the conscience of the heart. Having drunk that water then, the conscience being purged begins to live; and drinking in, it will have a fountain, will be itself a fountain. What is the fountain, and what is the river that flows from the belly of the inner man? Benevolence, whereby a

[30] Saint Augustine, Sermon 191, 4.
[31] Cf. Saint Augustine, *Expositions on the Psalms*, 76, 11.

man will consult the interest of his neighbor.... If he
is quick to consult for the good of his neighbor, then
he becomes not dry, because there is a flowing.... For
the fountain does not forsake us if we forsake not the
fountain.[32]

Having become dispensers of Christ's life, we must
be mediators of this infinite mercy and prove this state-
ment true: "Could God forget his mercy? The stream
flows, and should mercy dry up?" No, the pastor replies,
"It is easier for him to cease in his anger than in his
goodness."[33]

What a lesson! Ceaselessly meditating on chapter 25
of the Gospel of Saint Matthew, Augustine returns to it
more than 125 times in his preaching. He admits that he
is always moved by these words of Jesus: "Receive the
kingdom." Why will some receive the kingdom? "For
I was hungry and you gave me food." Why will others go into the eternal fire? "For I was hungry and you
gave me no food." Christ did not say: "Come, receive
the kingdom, for you were chaste, you never cheated
anyone, you were not unjust." He said: "Receive the
kingdom, for I was hungry and you gave me food."
Christ calls us to works of mercy.[34]

In fact, Augustine never stopped devoting himself to
the poor and the distressed of his diocese. He had a hospice built for the destitute. He even redeemed slaves.
Keeping only as much of his revenues as was necessary

---

[32] Saint Augustine, *Homilies on the Gospel of St. John*, XXXII, 4 [NPNF 1, 7:194a].

[33] Saint Augustine, *Expositions on the Psalms*, 76, 11.

[34] Ibid., 60, 9. Cf. J. Garcia, "La miséricorde d'après saint Augustin", *Con-naissance des Pères de l'Église* 139 (September 2015): 52–53.

for him and his clerics, he gave the rest to the poor. Christ therefore needs us. We should see this as a reason both of justice and of love, and as something necessary for our spiritual growth:

> In the person of the poor, he still needs you.... Besides, however opulent you may be, O rich man, you are only a beggar compared to God.... And yet Christ is not afraid to say to you: give me something of what I gave you.... I am the one who created everything that you have found here since your birth; you brought nothing.... Why do you not give me something of what I gave you?... You will give me a little, and I will repay you with much; for your earthly goods—heavenly goods; for your temporal goods—eternal goods.[35]

To give is to be enriched. While making me greater, works of mercy become a privileged way of enriching the Church, too, the Body of Christ, and "bridge of mercy". For "if you love the Head [Christ], you love the members, too."[36]

## MEDITATE WITH SAINT AUGUSTINE: THE GREATEST MERCY

In this sermon, Saint Augustine brings to light the apparent paradoxes taken up by the Word made flesh. He took on everything [about human nature], except sin, in order to join us even by his weaknesses:

[35] Saint Augustine, Sermon 124, III, 4.
[36] Saint Augustine, *Expositions on the Psalms*, 60, 6; Saint Augustine, *Homilies on the Gospel of St. John*, X, 3.

Now, what greater mercy is there than the one that
  caused the Creator of heaven to descend from
  heaven;
that clothed the Creator of earth in an earthly body;
that made our equal him who in eternity is equal to
  the Father;
that imposed the form of a slave on the Master of the
  world,
so that the Bread himself hungers,
and Fullness thirsts,
and Power is weakened,
and Health is wounded,
and Life is able to die?
And mercy does this so that our hunger might be
  stilled,
that our dryness might be watered,
that our weakness might be relieved,
that our iniquity might be blotted out,
that our charity might be inflamed.
What greater mercy is there than to see the Creator
  being created;
the Master becoming a slave;
the Redeemer being sold;
him who exalts being so utterly humiliated;
him who revives being killed?[37]

---

[37] Saint Augustine, Sermon 207, 1.

CHAPTER 9

# Love Both Christ and His Church

## THE CHURCH, "FULLNESS OF CHRIST"

Let us understand correctly the development of Augustine, who at the time of his conversion had summarized his goals as follows: "God and the soul, that is what I desire to know. Nothing more? Nothing whatsoever."[1] In that soul, finally a believer, a profound maturation took place that touched on the mystery of the Church. Soon Augustine would be able to say to his faithful flock: "Someone loves the Holy Spirit just as much as he loves the Church of Christ." Commenting on this passage, Joseph Ratzinger writes: "The measure of the Spirit coincides with the measure of one's fraternal love toward the community of the Lord's Body."[2]

The convert to Christ could not help but convert to the Church, because Augustine perceived that Jesus Christ and his Church are inseparable: "Will Christ, then, be alone in his house? Will no people remain at his

[1] Saint Augustine, *The Soliloquies*, I, 2, 7 [NPNF 1, 7:539a].

[2] Joseph Ratzinger, "L'Église dans la piété de saint Augustin" (written 1961), in: *Le Dieu de la foi et le Dieu des philosophes* (Paris: Parole et Silence, 2017), 147. Augustine is commenting on the Gospel of John (*Homilies on the Gospel of St. John*, XXIII, 8).

side? Whose head will he be, if there shall be no body?"
Yes, "the fullness of Christ, then, is head and members. Head and members, what is that? Christ and the Church."[3] Despite its apparent audacity, this "doctrine was largely incorporated in the development of Catholic dogma",[4] confirmed by the Magisterium of Pius XII in *Mediator Dei*, then at Vatican II. In the crucible of the battles to defend the Church, it is much to Augustine's credit that he was able to capture such a height.

This lesson touches something essential. Being Christians requires us to live grafted onto Christ in his Body, which is the Church. Thus "in him we are all christs and the Christ."[5] The Word assumed, so to speak, a "collective person", the man-Christ, Head of the Body made up of the baptized.

> The sons of God are the body of the only Son of God, and since he is the Head and we are the members, it is one Son of God. Therefore, he that loves the sons of God loves the Son of God.... Through love one comes to be in the frame of the Body of Christ, so that there shall be one Christ, loving himself.... You are therefore many, and you are one. How are we many and nevertheless only one? Because we are united to him whose members we are, and because our head is in heaven, so that his members might follow.[6]

[3] Saint Augustine, *Homilies on the Gospel of St. John*, XLI, 8, then XXI, 8 [NPNF 1, 7:232b and 140b].

[4] Yves Congar, "Introduction générale" to the *Traités anti-donatistes*, I, BA 28 (1963), 81.

[5] Saint Augustine, *Homilies on the Gospel of St. John*, CVIII, 5; Saint Augustine, *Expositions on the Psalms*, 26, 2, 2.

[6] Saint Augustine, *Homilies on the First Epistle of St. John*, X, 3 [NPNF 1, 7:521ab]; Saint Augustine, *Expositions on the Psalms*, 127, 4.

A distinction must be made, nevertheless, because salvation history is not finished. What Christ is as the glorious Head, we are not yet: we still toil on earth. Augustine loves to mention the *Christus totus*, Head and members, but he knows very well that only at the end of history will this whole Christ be unified in his fullness in the heavenly, eternal inheritance.[7]

## BUILDING UP THE CHURCH IN UNITY

In accepting the priesthood, Augustine understood that the contemplation resulting from his profound spiritual experience had to be offered and shared. He devoted himself without respite to the Church, that pastor of Hippo who wrote to the priest Eudoxius: "Do not prefer your own ease to the claims of the Church; for if no good men were willing to minister to her in her bringing forth of spiritual children, the beginning of your own spiritual life would have been impossible." When it is a question of the Church, our efforts are not in vain, because "you could not have for your sowing seasons a field more vast than Christ, who wanted us to sow on him. Your land is Christ."[8]

Augustine also sees the temple-church built of stones and wood as the image of the Church. Through our prayers, sacrifices, and sufferings, and united by the "cement of charity", we can become her living stones:

[7] See Saint Augustine, *Homilies on the Gospel of St. John*, XXVIII, 1; Saint Augustine, Sermon 22, 10.

[8] Saint Augustine, Letter to Eudoxius, 48, 2 [NPNF 1, 1:294b]; Saint Augustine, *Expositions on the Psalms*, 126, 11.

However, we become the house of the Lord only inasmuch as we are united by the cement of charity. If these stones and these beams were not joined together according to definite rules, if they did not embrace one another peacefully, if they did not love one another as they ought when they kissed each other, who would come into this place?... It is necessary, therefore, to achieve spiritually in our souls what we see in these material walls; and with God's grace to accomplish in our hearts what we see accomplished in these beams and these stones.[9]

The love of the Church! Do we want another proof of it? It is the way in which Augustine, perceiving the fragility of the Church in her members, invites them to preserve unity, not to let themselves be troubled by scandals, and not to abandon the "pastures of unity". The good and the bad are mixed in the Church; it is necessary to preserve unity even if the scandal comes from pastors, from priests: "Even as they follow the holy examples of the good shepherds who have gathered them, let the good sheep not put their hope in them but, rather, in the Lord who redeemed them with his blood."[10]

Love creates unity; love creates the whole Church. "Love this Church, be in this Church, be this Church."[11] If Augustine sees any disparity between Christ and his Church, this too is because of the sins of her members. The image of the Church as "Bride" is dear to him, because it expresses this tension of love that will be

---

[9] Saint Augustine, Sermon 336, 1 and 6.
[10] Saint Augustine, Letter 208, 6.
[11] Saint Augustine, Sermon 138, 10.

abolished only at the end of time, in the union and the holiness that are finally won: "When I talk about head and body, or about Bridegroom and Bride, understand the unique *unum* [one thing, i.e., Christ]. They appear to be two, but they are one. Love creates unity."[12]

Now African Christendom was torn at the time when Augustine became bishop. What had happened? During the last persecution of Christian antiquity around the years 303–304, Emperor Diocletian had ordered his police to confiscate the sacred books in all the churches. Some bishops yielded, others resisted and accused their colleagues of being *traditores* [Latin: those who hand over], or "traitors". Donatus, the dissident bishop of Carthage, organized a schism that would last for a century, in a climate of violence and sometimes of real terrorism. Carthage itself was half Donatist. This was an atrocious conflict between Christian brothers, within divided families; Augustine described it as follows: "Husbands and wives agree on matters concerning their bed but quarrel about matters concerning Christ's altar.... Parents and children have the same house, yet they do not have the same house of God."[13]

The Donatists defended a Church made up of the "pure". As for Augustine, he taught a *Catholica* [Catholic Church] that was truly *mixta* [mixed], with some bad members who are "in" the Church and yet are not "of" the Church.[14]

---

[12] Saint Augustine, Sermon 341, 10.

[13] Saint Augustine, Letter 33, 5.

[14] See Saint Augustine, *The City of God*, I, 35; Saint Augustine, Letter to Catholics about the Donatists, 8, 20, and 25, 75. However the wording "in/of" is not fixed, even though the thought is clear.

Augustine attempted dialogue, both spoken and written, proposed public debates, refuted error. When he died, the schism seemed to be healed. Augustine's suffering for his divided Church had stimulated his penetrating intellect, and his ecclesial doctrine sprang from a wounded heart: "Christ's inheritance encompasses the ends of the earth, and Christ's inheritance encompasses all the saints, and all the saints form only one man in Jesus Christ since unity is found in Jesus Christ; and this single man exclaims, 'From the ends of the earth I have cried to you, when my heart was in anguish.'"[15]

For Augustine, the unity of the Church—*unitas Ecclesiae*—appears as the synonym for the Body of Christ. Christ is one, "in his unity, his members, his body", one who cries out from the ends of the earth, who cries out from everywhere because he is "one man, Christ in his unity".[16] How many passages reflect this ardent thirst that Augustine had for unity, the kind that we will find only in Jesus Christ, the kind that is intact in him and divided in us!

When, as it may happen, some people suffer because of members of the Church or even through the actions of her leaders, Augustine begs us, he orders us not to disrupt unity. He asks us "to endure outrages and injustices patiently without disturbing the peace in the Church by the novelties of schism and heresy".[17] But sin demands justice, and Augustine had to punish sinful priests.

[15] Saint Augustine, *Expositions on the Psalms*, 120, 7.
[16] Ibid., 70, II, 4; 122, 2; 70, I, 6.
[17] Saint Augustine, *Treatise on the True Religion*, 6, 11.

## MARY, MOTHER OF UNITY AND
## MODEL OF THE CHURCH

Augustine sings the praises of a beautiful Church. He
sees the Virgin Mary as the house where the Father set
up the wedding bed for the union of the Word with the
Church his "Bride": "The womb of the Virgin Mary,
in which he became Head of the Church, was his bridal
chamber; from it he came forth as a bridegroom from
his chamber."[18] In explaining this relation between the
Church and the Virgin Mary, Augustine offered the
most original and richest side of his Marian spirituality;
we are rediscovering it today. In several beautiful passages, he affirms Mary's motherhood of the Church and
her role as "type" or model:

> You see, then, dearly beloved, you see how the Church
> is the Bride of Christ, which is obvious; likewise, she is
> the mother of Christ, which seems to us more difficult
> to understand and yet is no less true. The Virgin Mary
> was the type of the Church in advance. Now, I ask you,
> how is Mary the Mother of Christ, unless by the fact
> that she gave birth to Christ's members? Like Mary, this
> holy and glorious mother gives birth and remains a vir-
> gin.... Mary gave birth to your Head, but the Church
> gave birth to you, because the Church is simultaneously
> virgin and mother, mother by the bowels of charity,
> virgin by the integrity of her faith and piety.... Similar
> in this respect also to the Virgin who became for us all
> the mother of unity.[19]

[18] Saint Augustine, *Homilies on the Gospel of St. John*, VIII, 4 [NPNF 1,
7:58b]; cf. Saint Augustine, *Expositions on the Psalms*, 148, 8.
[19] Saint Augustine, Sermon 72A, 8 and then 192, 2.

The "mother of unity"! How can we not ask her prayers for the Church? Father Humann quite correctly remarks that Augustine gives Mary the beautiful title of "Star in the night"; he writes: "We can pray to Holy Mary to watch like a star in the night over our communities",[20] for their unity and for the unity of the Church.

Thus, we find in Mary a model for the Church, which is a spousal and maternal mystery, as Joseph Ratzinger recalled: "What we need, then, is to abandon this one-sided, Western activistic outlook.... This is why the Church needs the Marian mystery; this is why the Church herself is a Marian mystery. There can be fruitfulness in the Church only when she has this character, when she becomes holy soil for the Word. We must retrieve the symbol of the fruitful soil."[21]

Weighed down by the temptations of activism, the Church could very well be reduced to a "mere product of our activity and our planning".[22] Here we find a response to the risks of activism in communities or families that are involved in social service. Pope Francis recently echoed it: "The Church is not an NGO [a non-governmental organization]. It is a love story.... The Church is not in the first place an organization; she is Mother.... We are a family in the Church who is our Mother."[23]

[20] Fr.-M. Humann, *Règle de saint Augustin* (Paris: Salvator, 2016), 43.

[21] Joseph Ratzinger, in Joseph Ratzinger and Hans Urs von Balthasar, *Mary: The Church at the Source*, trans. Adrian Walker (San Francisco: Ignatius Press, 2005), 16–17.

[22] Joseph Ratzinger, "Le mystère de la Mère de Dieu", in *Le Ressuscité* (Paris: Desclée de Brouwer, 1986), 34.

[23] Pope Francis, Homily in Casa Santa Marta, April 24, 2013.

Indeed, there are ways of organizing Christian life that are much more functional and activist than maternal.

As Mother of the living, in Mary's image, the Church, too, must remain a virgin. For "Christ came, and he made his Church a virgin. She is a virgin by her faith.... Let her beware of the seducer, so as not to find him to be a corrupter. The Church is a virgin."[24] Hans Urs von Balthasar could write correctly: "Because Mary and the Church are virginal,... because both—to speak the language of the Old Testament—refuse adultery with idols or—to put it in contemporary language—resist the seduction of ideology, they are fruitful."[25]

Today, the idols can be found in fads, exclusivist identities, and theological or pastoral ideologies. Augustine invites us to a height and a wisdom that require great purity of intention.


## PRAYING AS CHURCH

The pastor of Hippo leads his people in the Church's prayer. He shows the connection between the soul of the believer, an individual and interior temple, and the immense temple of the whole Christ. It is indeed a living person whom the bishop introduces to his faithful flock, Christ praying in his members. Augustine daringly summons up the biblical words about the union of man and woman: Christ alone creates unity.

---

[24] Saint Augustine, Sermon 213, 7.
[25] Hans Urs von Balthasar, *Mary: The Church at the Source*, trans. Adrian Walker (San Francisco: Ignatius Press, 2005), 112.

Often in the psalms, Jesus Christ speaks in his own name, in his own person, which is our Head; and often, too, he speaks in the person of his Body, and we ourselves are this Body, the Church. But these different words always seem to come from the mouth of one man; so that we might understand correctly that the Head and the Body are one and the same whole and are not separated from one another; from this results the union about which it is said: "They shall be two in one flesh."[26]

Thus Augustine calls his faithful to make their own Christ's prayer in the Church, to speak *in* her, *through* her, but also *for* her, because she is the Body and "Bride" of Christ. In this ecclesial context, the liturgy could not set itself up as the self-manifestation of a community turned in on itself in the Africa of its time. On the contrary, all liturgy is open to the great *Ecclesia catholica*, in the "I" of the Body of Christ: "Here are your words, O Christ: 'I will proclaim you in the great assembly [*ecclesia*].' ... What is the great Church, my brethren? Can a minuscule part of the universe be the great Church? The great Church is the whole universe.... And you, you say that she subsists only in a remote corner!"[27]

## "SINGING IS A LOVER'S THING"

Here again we find the surge of Augustine's heart, moved by love: "Singing is a lover's thing."[28] The

---

[26] Saint Augustine, *Expositions on the Psalms*, 122, 2; 40, 1.
[27] Ibid., 21, II, 26.
[28] Saint Augustine, Sermon 336, 1.

liturgy in Milan, which he encountered when he was a catechumen, left him overwhelmed to the point of tears: "I see that our minds are more devoutly and earnestly inflamed in piety by the holy words when they are sung than when they are not."[29]

The bishop would always consider chant as being of primary importance for the liturgy of the Church. "The only time when the brothers who are assembled in church must not sing is when there is a reading, when someone is preaching, when the bishop prays aloud, or when the deacon announces common prayer."[30]

Is this not encouragement for everyone? Augustine commented—thousands of times, certainly—on the Gospels, letters, or psalms. He wants his listeners to enter more intimately into prayer and the liturgical texts. But also into the gestures: striking one's breast as a sign of repentance, prostrating oneself by making profound *metanias* as in the East, kneeling to pray as already was the custom at that time; he comments on words rich with meaning: *amen, alleluia, confiteor*, etc. In short, this model pastor wants to lead his flock toward the heights, through the symbolic liturgical signs and the sacred texts. Augustine must also impose liturgical silence, for his faithful sometimes prove to be noisy and undisciplined even in the basilica: "You go into your own house for temporal rest; you go into God's house for everlasting rest."[31]

Frederik van der Meer concludes that the bishop adds balance to his pedagogy.[32]

---

[29] Saint Augustine, *Confessions*, X, 33, 49.

[30] Saint Augustine, Letter 55, 34.

[31] Saint Augustine, *Homilies on the Gospel of St. John*, X, 9.

[32] Fr. van der Meer, *Saint Augustin, pasteur d'âmes* (Colmar-Paris: Alsatia, 1955), 2:71–116. This author describes extensively and precisely the liturgical atmosphere in Hippo.

This liturgical life also anticipates and prepares eternal life in which Christ, the sovereign priest, precedes us: "The subject of our meditation in this present life should be the praise of God; for the everlasting exultation of our life hereafter will be the praise of God, and no one can become fit for the life hereafter unless he practices for it now. This is indeed why we praise God even now."[33]

Here we have a feature of Augustinian spirituality: it is liturgical, nourished by the prayer of the Church. She makes her pilgrimage on earth toward the heavenly fatherland, and her liturgy leads us in hope.

MEDITATE WITH SAINT AUGUSTINE:
PRESERVING UNITY DESPITE SCANDALS

Saint Augustine writes to Felicia, a Christian woman who left the Donatist schism so as to enter the Catholic Church. Now she has painfully experienced the mediocrity of some Catholics, even of priests. Bishop Augustine does not conceal the reality of scandal, which will demand justice, but calls on her to preserve unity:

> I do not doubt, when I consider both your faith and the weakness or wickedness of others, that your mind has been disturbed.... Because in the body of our Lord Jesus Christ, in which all his members are one, you are very closely related to us, being loved as an honorable member in that body, and partaking with us of life in his Holy Spirit. I exhort you, therefore, not to be too much troubled by those scandals.... The Lord himself

---

[33] Saint Augustine, *Expositions on the Psalms*, 148, 1 [NPNF 1, 7:673a].

in his gospel foretold them.... There are, therefore, some who hold the honorable office of shepherds in order that they may provide for the flock of Christ; others occupy that position that they may enjoy the temporal honors and secular advantages connected with the office.... Just as there are good shepherds and bad shepherds, so also in flocks there are good and bad. The good are represented by the name of sheep, but the bad are called goats: they feed, nevertheless, side by side in the same pastures, and the Chief Shepherd, who is called the One Shepherd, shall come and separate them one from another according to his promise.... On us he has laid the duty of gathering the flock; to himself he has reserved the work of final separation, because it belongs properly to him who cannot err.... Our Shepherd himself wants us to remain in unity and that, although wounded by the scandals of those who are straw, we should not abandon the eagle's nest [l'aire] of the Lord.[34]

---

[34] Saint Augustine, Letter 208, 1–4 [NPNF 1, 1:558a–559a].

# CHAPTER 10

# The Community, "Sacrament" of the Trinity

Augustine does not want to go toward happiness alone but, rather, through Christ in his Church. Opening his heart in a commentary on the Psalms, he starts to pray, passing from "I" to "we", in other words, from himself to the Church: "'As the deer longs for running streams, so my soul longs for you, O God.' Who, then, is saying this? We ourselves, if only we are willing!... It is not, however, one individual, but it is one body: Christ's Body, or the Church.... Let us love together, let us thirst together, and let us run together to the sources of understanding."[1]

## THE COMMUNITY, MANIFESTATION OF TRINITARIAN UNITY

After his conversion, Augustine wanted to advance as a Christian with brethren in a form of common life. Cassiciacum, Milan, Thagaste, and Hippo are so many

---

[1] Saint Augustine, *Expositions on the Psalms*, 42, 1–2.

stages that enriched both his spiritual experience and his theology of communal life. For him, the desire for God takes a concrete ecclesial path: the community. The Church, which was born from the pierced side of Christ on the Cross, becomes visible for everyone at Pentecost. The first community in Jerusalem lived out this incorporation into the Body of Christ. It represents for Augustine the model that must be demonstrated by unity, prayer, and common ownership of goods: "To let you know where Scripture describes the form of life that we want to imitate, we will read to you a passage from the Acts of the Apostles."[2]

Augustine then speaks about community in the same terms that are used to describe the Church. For the task of Augustinian common life is to make visible the ecclesial body, to "practice in miniature" what the *Catholica* lives at large, in short, to be "the Mystical Body of Christ on a small scale".[3]

Augustine goes farther. He tries to show that the community must have "one heart and one soul" in order to be, to "embody", the mystery of the Church in a manifestation of the unity of the Trinity: "The Father and the Son willed to gather us *in unum* [into one] through this gift who is the Holy Spirit."[4] The Holy Spirit is the one who acts to make this union possible, as at Pentecost. The Father and the Son willed that we be in communion among ourselves and with them through what they have in common: the Holy Spirit. He is the "unity

[2] Saint Augustine, Sermon 356, 1; cf. Acts 2:42–44; 4:32.
[3] J. Garcia, *Expérience de Dieu et communauté: Suivre le Christ à l'école de saint Augustin* (Paris: Cerf, 1994), 101.
[4] Saint Augustine, Sermon 71, 18.

of the Father and of the Son", the gift common to the Father and the Son, which can be called friendship or else charity, Saint Augustine declares.[5]

Our participation in the Trinitarian unity is clearly expressed in the Gospel: "That they may be one even as we are one" (Jn 17:22–23); and Jesus insists that this "as" is not a mere comparison but, rather, a participation: "I in them and you in me, that they may become perfectly one." The divine plan commands the manifestation of this Trinitarian unity, through a participation by Christians. This manifestation was realized by the early Church: "[They] were of one heart and soul, ... and they had everything in common" [Acts 4:32]. The intention of Augustinian common life is to give flesh to this exegesis, to incarnate this manifestation of Trinitarian unity *through* and *in* ecclesial unity.

Note that this doctrine, which is especially implemented by canonial life, harmonizes with the efforts of the Magisterium, which refers to consecrated life as a sign of the Church. Its current relevance lies also in the fact that Christian culture is disappearing, Christian rituals are becoming too discreet, since the social weight of Western Catholicism is approaching zero. "So much so", Father Dauzet says, "that Christians have a new need to see, feel, and touch their Church. It is necessary to make the body visible. This is the task of our canonial communities today."[6] "Only One is almighty, the Trinity which is one God, the one thing necessary (*unum*

[5] Saint Augustine, *On the Trinity*, VI, 5, 7.

[6] D.-M. Dauzet, *Vie canoniale, vie féminine, sanctification dans l'ordre de Prémontré*, International Conference of the Sisters of the Premonstratensian Order, Berne Abbey, Netherlands, August 2009.

*necessarium*, Lk 10:42). Nothing leads us to this one thing but to have one heart, however numerous we may be."[7]

Augustine insists: unity of hearts is the way to enter into participation in the Trinitarian unity. The charity that unites leads us to see and to experience this Trinitarian mystery. Recall Augustine's teaching: "You see the Trinity if you see charity." "To see" means to experience, to perceive with the heart the richness of the gift, the unity of persons who are bound by true charity.[8] The desire for God has become unity.

These communities, these *ecclesiolae* [little churches], can be instituted at various levels: canonial communities (abbeys, monasteries), Augustinian apostolic communities, etc. Families, too, can be grafted onto this living vine. We are deeply convinced of this, because Augustine refers to the family as a "domestic church", using comparable expressions for both the community and the Christian home.[9]


THE EUCHARIST, SACRAMENT OF OUR UNITY

Fervent Christians who consider the Eucharist in its individual effects rightly see in it a means of growing in union with God. This is true, but insufficient. Augustine helps us to situate the Eucharist again in its essential place: confected by the Church as "bread of concord",

---

[7] Saint Augustine, Sermon 103, III, 4.

[8] Saint Augustine, *On the Trinity*, VIII, 7, 12; Saint Augustine, *Homilies on the First Epistle of St. John*, VII, 10.

[9] Saint Augustine, together with Saint John Chrysostom, originated this expression, "the domestic church".

the Eucharist builds up the unity of the community that is gathered around the altar. From this Eucharistic source, families, parishes, or religious communities draw their life of unity and their strength. For Augustine, the Eucharist is assuredly the sacrament of unity:

> "One bread." What is this bread? "One body." Recall that one and the same bread is not formed from one grain of wheat but from many. At the moment of the exorcisms, you were in a way under the millstone; at the moment of baptism, you became a lump of dough; and you were baked in a way when you received the fire of the Holy Spirit. Be what you see, and receive what you are.... Here are many grapes hanging in a cluster; soon they will be only one juice. This then is the model that Christ our Lord gave us; this is the way in which he willed to unite us to his person. He consecrated at his table the mystery of our peace and of our unity.[10]

There is nothing less individualistic than this! Augustinian spirituality is in one sense totally Eucharistic. The many grains of wheat, Augustine says, are "united after being ground". Thus the sufferings of common life—whether in religion or in the family—crush us, and we pass through the fire of charity that is given by the Holy Spirit. Community difficulties are not in vain, far from it: they then become part of the realization of the mystery of unity, signified sacramentally by the Eucharist: "You are what you have received."[11] Our faith opens up immense perspectives every day.

---

[10] Saint Augustine, Sermon 272 (cf. also Saint Augustine, Sermon Deny 6, 2: "What is to come is One, therefore you be one also.")

[11] Saint Augustine, Sermon 227.

FRIENDSHIP IN CHRIST

In Augustine's life, friendship had a privileged place, and he never rejected it. Through his successive foundations, his theology of friendship widened and deepened in contact with the mystery of Christ, the foundation of the communion of persons. This friendship had philosophical roots stated by Cicero, but here it is made supernatural by the gift of charity: "Friendship is a benevolent, affectionate conformity of opinions about divine and human matters."[12]

In Augustine's relationships, therefore, an art of living flourishes, made up of kindness, courtesy in friendship, and a *humanitas* that gives a cordial note to every exchange: "There must be not only charity between us; there must also be the freedom of friendship", he writes to Saint Jerome.[13] That, however, was no easy thing between those two strong personalities!

What is the place of friendship? Can we enjoy it or simply use it? "Of all things, only friendship and health are desirable for their own sakes.... These are the two necessary goods in this world: health and a friend; the rest is superfluous."[14]

Yes, we can enjoy friendship, "but in God". For friendship in God develops into communion, "a spiritual embrace", and becomes a "dear and sweet bond because of the unity that it achieves between the souls".[15] This

---

[12] Saint Augustine, Letter 258, 1; cf. Saint Augustine, *Confessions*, IV, 4, 7.
[13] Saint Augustine, Letter 82, 35.
[14] Saint Augustine, Letter 130, 13.
[15] Saint Augustine, Sermon 299 D, 1; Saint Augustine, *On the Trinity*, IX, 8, 13; Saint Augustine, *Confessions*, II, 5, 10.

friendship is evangelized by Christ's grace: "For there is no true friendship save between those [whom] you [O Lord] bind together and who are united to each other by that love which is 'shed abroad in our hearts through the Holy Spirit who is given to us'."[16]

Only a friendship founded on Christ will remain solid and pure. In him alone "can it find furthermore eternity and happiness."[17]

It is good for a religious community—or for a family, to differing degrees—to adopt Augustine's doctrine and experience as its own. But this friendship must be profoundly purified. Writing to Bishop Paulinus of Nola, Augustine mentions his friend Romanius: "Beware of believing all the good that my friend may tell you about me. I have often noticed that, without intending to lie but being carried away by his heart, he erred in his judgment and thought that I possessed some gifts that I lack."[18]

True friendship in Christ, then, causes souls and the community itself to grow. Augustine sketches a very tactful picture of it:

> To discourse and jest with him; to indulge in courteous exchanges; to read pleasant books together; to trifle together; to be earnest together; to differ at times without ill-humor, as a man might do with himself, and even through these infrequent dissensions to find zest in our more frequent agreements; sometimes

[16] Saint Augustine, *Confessions*, IV, 4, 7.
[17] Saint Augustine, Letter 258, 4; Saint Augustine, *Against Two Letters by the Pelagians*, I, 1, 11.
[18] Saint Augustine, Letter 27, 4.

teaching, sometimes being taught; longing for someone absent with impatience and welcoming the home-
comer with joy.[19]

We all know how much sin can compromise unity,
weaken communities of life, whether lay or religious.
Augustine is a realist. When someone asked him: "What
would happen if you could not manage to persuade
your brethren to live amicably?" he answered: "I would
bear with them as well as I could, and for their part
they would do the same!" He was acquainted with those
severe efforts to practice the patient charity that bears
with another's imperfections. The community becomes
a "furnace" that consumes the utopian dreams of perfect
peace.[20] Through charity, nevertheless, the fire of the
Holy Spirit, the metals that clash can be melted into one
beautiful metal.


## A RULE FOR COMMUNITIES

We understand better what led Augustine to found
communities: love for unity in charity, the desire to
manifest the Trinitarian communion, friendship in
Christ. These major lines of impetus are found, explic-
itly or between the lines, in the rule that Augustine
wrote around the year 397. As a bishop, he had left his
first monastery in Hippo to live in the bishop's residence; he left this rule for his brothers. For some nuns,

[19] Saint Augustine, *Confessions*, IV, 8, 13.
[20] Saint Augustine, *The Soliloquies*, I, 12, 20, and *Expositions on the Psalms*,
99, 11.

too, he would adapt the text, written in the feminine but basically identical.

We find in it the theme of unity in charity: "Live harmoniously in the house [Ps 68:6] and to have one heart and one soul seeking God" (Rule 1, 2). In this mutual charity dwells a "spiritual beauty" that must be desired and loved, that becomes a witness to offer to the world (Rule 8, 1). Common life in charity is not a fringe benefit or a mere means, but an essential component of their life, in a communal journey toward God, *in Deum*. Indeed, "Let us love together, let us thirst together, and let us run together to the sources of understanding." A note of joyful simplicity should resound in this familial group.[21] The search for happiness, which has been emphasized since the beginning of our study, is revealed in this itinerary of sanctity.

The rule prescribes, furthermore, adapting to the needs of each person, whether sick or well, strong or weak. "Your superior ought to provide each of you with food and clothing, not on an equal basis to all, because all do not enjoy the same health, but to each one in proportion to his need" (Rule 1, 3).

Augustinian poverty consists of placing all goods in common: "Do not call anything your own; possess everything in common" (Rule 1, 3), in imitation of the first community in Jerusalem. For Saint Augustine, this poverty is at the foundation of unity that gathers everyone in charity; it is the tangible sign thereof. Witnessing to the primacy of the common good, it demands a

---

[21] Saint Augustine, *Expositions on the Psalms*, 41, 2; cf. A. Trapè, *La Règle de saint Augustin commentée* (Bégrolles-en-Mauges: Bellefontaine, 1993), 117.

struggle against the selfish ego. This is indeed another element of Augustinian asceticism, in the service of unifying charity: "The Scriptures tell us: 'Love is not self-seeking.' We understand this to mean: the common good takes precedence over the individual good, the individual good yields to the common good" (Rule 5, 2). This is an asceticism of care, mutual support, and renunciation of the idolatry of the ego; it is a beautiful and demanding prophetic sign for our times, which are characterized by individualism.

The role of the superior is of capital importance if the community is to grow in this common sanctity. Augustine's teaching about authority, a service of love, *servitium amoris*, obviously must be applied in the community family: "Your superior should regard himself to be fortunate as one who serves you in love, not as one who exercises authority over you. Accord him the first place of honour among you, but in fear before God he shall lie prostrate beneath your feet" (Rule 7, 3).

We have seen that the community must manifest the Trinitarian communion. This is why Augustine wants to call the religious "monks", because of their union in Christ thanks to the gift which is the Holy Spirit. If they make the words of Scripture a reality—"one heart and one soul"—they can be called "monks" because they are "one":

But then why would we too not call our members "monks", since the Psalm says: "Behold, how good and pleasant it is when brothers dwell in unity, *in unum*"? *Monos* [in Greek], in fact, means "one", *unum* [in Latin], and not just "one or an" in any sense.... Therefore those who live in unity, *in unum*, in such a way that they make up one man, in such a way that in them is fulfilled what is written: "one soul and one heart"—from many bodies, but not from many souls, from many bodies, but not from many hearts—they are rightly called *monos*, in other words "a single one", *unum*.[22]

This beautiful definition has to be explained. In designating a canon regular or an Augustinian religious by the name of "monk", we understand that it is not in the same way as a Benedictine monk or a Carthusian. With Augustine, the perspective becomes ecclesial, marked by the desire for unity. Not fusion—which in fact would be a confusion—but truly unity in the diversity of temperaments, origins, talents. Harmony becomes an expression of unity.

This spirituality has nourished religious communities for centuries, but it can also inspire Christian families, which are real "domestic churches". It adds dynamism to the effort to be holy while traveling toward eternity, where the *unum*, our oneness, will no longer be hindered by the divisions of our sins.

MEDITATE WITH SAINT AUGUSTINE:
JUSTICE AND FORGIVENESS

In this passage from his rule, Augustine gives instruction about justice and forgiveness. In it we can admire his sense of balance as well as his concrete demands. Justice is inseparable from charity; it is the first path of charity,

---

[22] Saint Augustine, *Expositions on the Psalms*, 133, 6.

its "minimum requirement". But charity surpasses justice and completes it in the logic of the gift and forgiveness. For families, whether religious or lay, this teaching
is of capital importance:

> Whoever has offended another with insults or harmful
> words, or even a serious accusation, must remember
> to right the wrong he has done at the earliest oppor-
> tunity. The injured must remember to forgive without
> further bickering. If they have offended each other,
> they shall mutually forgive their offences for the sake of
> your prayers [i.e., the Lord's Prayer, the Our Father].
> The more frequent your prayers are, the sounder they
> ought to be. An individual who is prone to anger, yet
> hastens to beg forgiveness from someone he has con-
> sciously harmed, is better than another who is less
> inclined to anger and less likely to ask pardon. An indi-
> vidual who absolutely refuses to ask pardon, or does so
> without meaning it, is entirely out of place in the mon-
> astery, even if he is not dismissed. Spare yourselves the
> use of words too harsh. If they have escaped your lips,
> those same lips should promptly heal the wounds they
> have caused. (Rule 6, 2)

# Chapter 11

# En Route to the Kingdom

## HOLINESS OF HARMONY

Love of God and love of neighbor, contemplation, and apostolate. Throughout his life and his teaching, Augustine challenges us: Are harmony and peace possible? This bishop, who was ceaselessly hard at work and consumed by his responsibilities, had to do an apprenticeship in the holiness of harmony. Unity came to be in him at the deepest level: going to God with others, for others, through others. He lived what Saint Thomas Aquinas would express later on: "It is a sign of greater love if a man devotes himself to others for his friend's sake than if he be willing only to serve his friend."[1] Charity builds up an equilibrium, despite the inevitable psychological tensions. It unites. In a famous passage, Augustine explains:

> No man has a right to lead such a life of contemplation as to forget in his own ease the service due to his neighbor; nor has any man a right to be so immersed in active life as to neglect the contemplation of God.... Love

[1] Thomas Aquinas, *Summa Theologiae*, II–II, q. 184, art. 7 ad 2.

141

of the truth is motive enough to embrace the holy leisure of contemplation, but charity and necessity should be our motives for engaging in activity, so that if no one imposes this burden upon us, we are free to devote ourselves to the search for the truth and the contemplation thereof; but if it is a duty imposed on us, we must submit to it out of charity and necessity.[2]

As we saw earlier, what was at stake for Augustine the bishop was to harmonize *otium* and *negotium*. *Otium* is holy, contemplative "leisure" dedicated to the search for God; *negotium* is activity, pastoral responsibilities. Now Augustine experienced a deep and lasting peace of soul. He wrote then to Nebridius: "Believe me, one needs to withdraw completely from the tumult of passing things in order to achieve true fearlessness—without becoming either dull or rash. This is the basis of lasting joy, with which no pleasure can compare.... How is it that this peace accompanies a man even in the business of life, if he goes forth to his duties from this sanctuary?"[3]

Augustine answers: Truly interior prayer, in the solitude of the soul, can give rise to this unity and this peace, even in the midst of activity. In God who is loved, the gift unifies being. Charity bears a very beautiful fruit: peace.

Augustine often meditated on the two Gospel figures of Martha and Mary: they symbolize the active life and the contemplative life. Do not set these two sisters in opposition, but look at how they live in harmony! Like Mary, we must listen and contemplate; like Martha, we must give, offer, and serve. Martha, figure of labor in

---

[2] Saint Augustine, *The City of God*, XIX, 19 [cf. NPNF 1, 2:413b].
[3] Saint Augustine, Letter 10, 2–3 [NPNF 1, 1:228b].

the present life, must accompany Mary, figure of that future life which is anticipated by contemplation.

In the charity that unites, the bishop, in fact, found an equilibrium and a peace that blossom in renunciation. Commenting on a psalm, he writes: "You sang the psalms as much as you could, and then you withdrew. But let your soul continue to make the praises of God resound. You are conducting your business: let your soul praise the Lord." Augustine proposes a form of holiness common to lay people in the world and to apostolic religious; it presupposes an equilibrium—which must ceaselessly be reevaluated—between prayer and action. Renunciation becomes a "plan of action": "If anything unavoidable happens that interferes with the plan that we have proposed, we should bend ourselves to it readily instead of being discouraged, as we should adopt the plan that God has preferred to our own. It is more fitting that we should follow God's will than that he should follow ours.... The true plan of action is to resolve never to fight against God's power."[4]

Saint Paul VI expressed this Augustinian harmony nicely: "He appears to us as such a lively, universal good soul, such an admirable interpreter of the two worlds that we have to unite—man's and God's—that we feel a very special veneration for him." According to the pope, the writings of Augustine "are the deep, calm source of living, gushing water, which is necessary in order to direct our life on the twofold way of the apostolate for the sake of souls and the preeminence of union with God."[5]

---

[4] Saint Augustine, *Catechism of the Uninstructed*, 14, 20 [NPNF 1, 3:297b].
[5] Paul VI, Address on December 14, 1966, and Address on March 20, 1971.

144

"THE TIMES ARE WHAT WE ARE"

Saint Augustine gave to his faithful living in the world some clear guidelines for their conduct. Many pagans still lived among the population. Their spectacles, violent games, and indecent ways of life could tempt some Christians. Augustine encouraged his flock to be "in" the world and not "of" the world. He wanted a separation in spirit, in other words, rejecting what the world believes, hoping not for the "frivolities of this age but eternal life with Christ", loving the Creator of the world, whereas the pagans "love only the world". It is necessary "to prove it by one's life, to show it by one's actions". If this is the case, then have no fear: "Separated spiritually, do not fear to be among them in a bodily way.... This separation consists of leading a life different from that of the pagans, while remaining externally in their midst."[6]

The Christian must "redeem the time" because these days seem to be bad, but to do so by toiling in time. This may mean the sacrifice of material advantages. Augustine gives several concrete examples to his faithful: for instance, to give up some material gains in a trial or in a matter of inheritance, if that could result in more time for God or some other spiritual advantage. Always with prudence, obviously.[7]

These, therefore, are requirements for the life of laymen, conditions for their positive influence on the world. Neither isolation or sectarianism, nor "dilution" by choices that are opposed to the Gospel. Augustine

[6] Saint Augustine, Sermon 198, 2.
[7] Saint Augustine, Sermon 167, 3.

does not mince words: far from being dangerous to society, "the sincere practice of Christianity is the greatest guarantee of safety" for the nations. In its flexibility, Christianity can adapt to a diversity of customs and institutions, since nothing is opposed to the search for peace and to the worship of God.[8]

We must live out this ideal in the present active tense. For history has not come to its conclusion; the present moment is still the time of pilgrimage. The era here below is the time of combat and hope.

When the Roman Empire was thoroughly decadent, Augustine taught the faithful to live in a time of crisis: "Alas, evils would not multiply so much if the wicked were not so numerous! The times are bad, the times are difficult, everyone says. Let us live well, and the times will be good. We are the ones who make the time; it is as we are."[9]

What a lesson! When confronted with pessimism or bitterness, the Christian should set the tone and give the "pitches" tuned to hope and charity.

Thus our very struggles should still be measured by this charity. Augustine recalls that the Holy Spirit descended in the form of a dove in order to pour out charity into our hearts. Why? A dove has no gall, but she defends her nest with her beak and claws. If she has to injure someone, "she does it without being harsh."[10]

Let us join our voices but above all our hearts in the service of these labors. Prayer in common and the Church's liturgy nourish and strengthen souls in the battles of the

---

[8] Saint Augustine, Letter 138, 15; Saint Augustine, *The City of God*, XIX, 17.
[9] Saint Augustine, Sermon 80, 8.
[10] Saint Augustine, *Homilies on the First Epistle of St. John*, VII, 11.

pilgrimage. "If you love, you sing. We must therefore sing and praise the Lord, because song helps us to overcome the difficulties along the way."[11]

Places where the Christian liturgy is celebrated are oases where hope takes root.


## TOWARD THE CITY OF GOD

The Christian must live already by the principles of the City of God, which Augustine contrasts with the City here below, the Earthly City. The foundation of the latter is pride, ambition, "love of self even to disdain for God—it demands its glory from men."[12] The City of God is not a "ghetto" but expresses a spirit, a spiritual attitude based on the virtues, charity, and God's sovereignty. These two cities indicate, therefore, a way of life: one builds on perishable goods, the other counts on God. Let us look carefully at them: these two cities are tangled up until the end of the world. For here below, the weeds are mixed in with the good wheat, even in the Church, where unity must still be perfected. And the City of God will live in perfect concord only at the end of its itinerary:

> We are all called to form one City, having one soul and one heart for God. After death, this unity will become such that the most intimate thoughts will be perceived

[11] Saint Augustine, Sermon 255, I.
[12] Saint Augustine, *The City of God*, XIV, 28.

by everyone, without encountering the least diver-
gence anywhere.... This unity will arrive at its perfection when the darkness has unveiled its secrets, when
all the thoughts of the heart have been manifested and
everyone will receive his praise from God.[13]

Charity will have reached its fullness. The City of
God will be the community perfectly ordered and harmonious "in the enjoyment of God and mutual enjoyment in God".[14] Until then, we are pilgrims, going
forward together toward eternity.

But when death has been swallowed up in His victory,
these evils will no longer exist; they will give way to a
complete and endless peace.... Who would not sigh
after this happy City where no friend leaves, where no
enemy comes in, where there is neither temptation nor
sedition nor schism in the people of God, no instrument of the devil to afflict the Church?... A perfect
peace will reign therefore among the children of God,
who will love one another, will see themselves filled
with God, for God will be all in all. Therefore it is God
whom we will all see, God whom we will all possess,
God who will be peace for all of us.[15]

Then we will have fulfilled our desires in the unity
of one and the same family. Satisfied with joy, we will
have found the source of all desire and of all unity: the
Trinity.

[13] Saint Augustine, *The Good of Marriage*, 18, 21.
[14] Saint Augustine, *The City of God*, XIX, 13.
[15] Saint Augustine, *Expositions on the Psalms*, 84, 10.

MEDITATE WITH SAINT AUGUSTINE:
THE ALLELUIA OF THE ROAD AND
THE ALLELUIA OF THE FATHERLAND

The liturgy has us sing the alleluia. This is because if
we members of the Church are to take courage and to
advance in hope, we must do so together:

> Our life is a pilgrimage toward our fatherland, and if
> we are walking toward it, this is because we love it.
> Now when you love, you sing. We must therefore sing
> and praise the Lord, because singing helps us to over-
> come the difficulties along the way. Singing gives us the
> strength and courage to continue to walk on the Lord's
> road.... Today the alleluia is the traveler's canticle: by
> a difficult path we are heading for the peaceful father-
> land where all activity will have ceased and our sole
> occupation will be alleluia.... Here hope prompts us to
> sing; there the motive will be enjoyment. Here it is the
> alleluia of the road; there—the alleluia of the fatherland.
> Today, then, my brethren, let us sing, not yet to delight
> in our rest, but to ease our burden.... Sing and walk.
> What does it mean to walk? Advance, make progress in
> the good; for as the Apostle says, there are those who
> progress in evil, going from bad to worse [2 Tim 3:13].
> For you, too, this walking is a form of progress, but may
> it be progress in the good, progress in right faith, prog-
> ress in purity of life. Sing and walk, without taking the
> wrong road, without going backward, without coming
> to a standstill: sing and walk![16]

---

[16] Saint Augustine, Sermon 255, 1; 256, 3.

# CONCLUSION

Saint Augustine encountered God, and the experience to which he testifies is above all the encounter with a person, Jesus Christ. This encounter turned his life upside down, just as it changes the lives of those women and men who in every age have the grace to encounter Christ in his truth and his mercy.

In the designs of Providence, Augustine was led to bring the Christian message to the simple folk. A profound intention guided him throughout his life as a bishop: reject the temptation to compose major theological treatises, because "it is more urgent to have texts that, we hope, will be useful to a great number of people."[1] Communicating the faith in a way that everyone could understand seemed to him more urgent. But for him, this was a true sacrifice, and today we are the fortunate beneficiaries of it.

You agreed to follow Augustine in these pages. We hope that we have successfully carried out our plan: to introduce a man whose faith is "fresh and relevant", words that have scarcely aged, writings that reveal the lasting relevance of the faith that we have received from Christ; and thus to ascend with the bishop of Hippo toward the fatherland, the Holy Trinity. These pages then will have been not so much an object of study

---

[1] Saint Augustine, Letter 169, 1, 1.

as spiritual nourishment. In skimming together through these texts by Augustine, we will have rediscovered the difference between studying a musical score and enjoying the music that it contains.

Augustine leads us to advance as a community, in the Church that we love as she is, because "love brings us into the cohesion of the Body of Christ." This seeker of truth asks us to proclaim it by our words and by our whole lives. But as a doctor of charity, he invites us to give everything in love, because "only the truth will win the victory, and the victory of truth is charity."[2]

The strong words of this bishop, spoken in difficult times, nourish our souls and encourage us to go forward in hope as more peaceful, more radiant Christians. For hope, as Augustine said quite correctly, is "the source of all our joys".

---

[2] Saint Augustine, *Expositions on the Psalms*, 127, 4; Saint Augustine, Sermon 358, 1.

# APPENDIX

## Augustine among Us

### SAINT AUGUSTINE: WHERE CAN WE READ HIM?

Saint Isidore of Seville, an immensely erudite Father of the Church, once said ironically that if a man boasted of having read all the works of Augustine, he would be a liar. No doubt this is an exaggeration. Nevertheless, when confronted with such a vast corpus of works, beginners sometimes get discouraged. Well, then, where to start?

It makes sense to begin with the *Confessions*. Note that this is more than the autobiography of a convert; it is already a theological work, which Augustine composed when he was bishop and had been baptized for ten years. Except for a few passages or chapters, the book is easy to read, and there are numerous editions in English, even in paperback.

The reader could continue with anthologies of excerpts from our saint, published by various editors. Some are voluminous, while others are very slim, offering variations on a single theme or else selections on a variety of topics. The *Homilies on the First Epistle of St. John* could follow, then a selection from the *Homilies on the Gospel of St. John,* or from the admirable *Expositions on the Psalms.* Similarly, his *Sermons* are becoming accessible in French in several editions.

Little by little, all of Augustine's writings are being published in English by New City Press in the series: The Works of Saint Augustine: A Translation for the 21st Century (WSA). As of this writing, forty-four of a projected forty-nine volumes are in print. This important edition replaces many English translations that were inaccurate or in archaic language.

We can meet Augustine on the worldwide web, too:

www.augustinus.de: site of the *Augustinus Lexikon.*

http://www.augustinus.it: all the works of Augustine in Latin and an Italian translation, with an essay on the iconography of Saint Augustine.

http://www.osabel.be: the Augustinian center in Leuven.

http://www.documentacatholicaomnia.eu.

http://www.bibliotheque=monastique.ch/bibliotheque/bibliotheque/sacrits/augustin: digitized versions of the nineteenth-century French translations of Augustine (with Abbé Raulx as editor-in-chief: a less literal translation than in the scholarly Latin-French edition *La Bibliothèque augustinienne* [BA], but very elegant).

http://www.ccel.org/fathers: Online version of Nicene and Post-Nicene Fathers, Series 1. Volumes 1 through 8 include most of Augustine's major works in nineteenth-century Protestant translations of very uneven quality.

## SAINT AUGUSTINE: WHERE CAN WE STUDY HIM?

There are countless books that study the thought of Augustine and comment on his teaching. A bibliography by Franz Mali shows that more than one scholarly book or article on Saint Augustine has appeared every other day over the past ten years! And the researcher admits that it is quite difficult to list them all.

Within the context of this introductory book, we have reduced as much as possible the references to the secondary literature, mentioning almost exclusively in the footnotes current books that are easily accessible—sometimes from second-hand booksellers—to a motivated public of non-theologians.

Among these texts, let us not forget those of the Magisterium: thus, Saint John Paul II published the beautiful Apostolic Letter *Augustine of Hippo* on August 28, 1986, while Benedict XVI offered a series of substantial audiences in 2008.

In French, the saint is accessible to everyone, in different genres; a children's book version of his life is available: *Saint Augustin: Si tu savais le don de Dieu* [If you knew the gift of God], by Dominique Bar. The canonesses in Azille published a compact disc of their chanting: *Saint Augustin: À la recherche du bonheur*; on several tracks, veteran French actor Roland Giraud gives profound readings of passages by Augustine, demonstrating how timeless they are.

Returning to the field of French scholarship, we emphasize the work done for many years by the Institut d'études augustiniennes (IEA, Institute for Augustinian

Studies). It has produced several series of books: the Bibliothèque augustinienne (BA), which is the standard edition of the works of Saint Augustine in the French-speaking world (edited Latin text and translation, accompanied by substantial notes); the Nouvelle Bibliothèque augustinienne (NBA), providing the translation alone in paperback format. For those who want to study the material in greater depth, the IEA publishes the scholarly series "Études augustiniennes" as well as two periodicals: *Revue d'études augustiniennes et patristiques* and *Recherches augustiniennes et patristiques*.

## SAINT AUGUSTINE: WHERE CAN WE SEE HIM AND EXPERIENCE HIM?

Saint Augustine influenced all of Western religious life, and a great many religious follow his rule, while others were inspired by it. Both the number and the variety of these heirs make it difficult to compile an exhaustive list. Indeed, to date no author has attempted it.

### Heirs of the Patristic Era: Canons and Canonesses Regular

From the eleventh century on, the Rule of Saint Augustine was required of religious clerics who served the Church and the faithful. The first documented instance of a community following this rule is the community of canons of the cathedral of Maguelone in southern France, in 1095.

These communities form the order of canons regular; some of its congregations are recent, others are reconnecting today with this charism. They all have in common a stable way of life, centered on the liturgy and fraternal charity and regular service to the faithful. Hence their life is very close to that of Augustine himself. There is a feminine form of this life, too, in contemplative or apostolic communities. As we mentioned, although canonesses and canons regular were driven out of France after the Revolution, they are reviving today.[1]

Among them we find, in French-speaking countries: the Canons of Prémontré, with their abbeys in Mondaye and Frigolet, in Belgium in Leffe, the Priory in Conques (there are many Premonstratensians as well as the Norbertine Sisters on several continents); the Canons of Latran (in France, a house in Notre-Dame de Beauchêne, canons and canonesses present in the world); in Switzerland, the Canons of Saint-Maurice d'Agaune (who run a large secondary school there) have been influential for centuries, along with the Canons of Grand Saint-Bernard, whose charism is hospitality, at the hospice by the same name or at the Simplon Pass; the Congregation of Saint Victor—canons and canonesses—with their abbey in Champagne-sur-Rhône and priories in Montbron, Chancelade, and Bourg-lès-Valence; the Canons and Canonesses of Windesheim exist outside of France; the teaching Canonesses of the Congregation of Notre-Dame, whose best-known school bears the name "Les Oiseaux" (The Birds); the nursing Canonesses of the Mercy of Jesus, of which the most famous is Malestroit; the Canons of the Immaculate Conception,

---

[1] Mondaye Abbey hosted two colloquia on canonial life: D.-M. Dauzet, ed., *La Voie canoniale dans l'Église aujourd'hui*, Vie consacrée 9 (Namur, 1994); H. Vermes, ed., *La Vie canoniale aujourd'hui: Communauté et mission sous la règle de saint Augustin* (Paris: Parole et Silence, 2015).

present in Charroux (but they have several houses outside of France); the Canons of Mary Mother of the Redeemer, in La Cotellerie; the Canons and Canonesses Regular of the Mother of God, respectively in Lagrasse Abbey and the monastery in Azille.

This list shows a living canonial charism; it is already long but not exhaustive, and we would have to add institutes outside of the French-speaking world.

### The Order of Saint Augustine, the Medieval Orders, and the Assumptionists

The mainstream of the Order of Saint Augustine is still alive. We have mentioned the hermits of Saint Augustine, to which several branches are attached; those who are also called simply Augustinians are not represented in France by communities of men. On the other hand, in France there are a dozen apostolic institutes of the great family of Augustinian Sisters, who are devoted mainly to the sick, the poorest of the poor, and education. Outside of France, the Augustinian Sisters were able to assume more strictly contemplative forms (Saint Rita of Cascia is the best known example of them).

In the 1850s, Father d'Alzon founded the "Family of the Assumption", which has one male institute—the Augustinians of the Assumption—and five female congregations. Their charism makes them suited for various works of teaching (the Assumptionist Fathers have houses in France, particularly in university cities), mission work, service to the poor, media apostolates, and theological research (they are active with the Institut d'Études Augustiniennes [IEA], which was mentioned above).

Some medieval Orders follow the Rule of Saint Augustine, but with a specific pastoral vocation: we mention especially the Dominicans, the Order of Preachers. Others devote themselves to education or care for the sick (and at one time to ransoming captives and defending the Holy Places). Thus, in the twelfth century, John of Matha founded the Trinitarians to ransom captives, and today Trinitarian Brothers and Sisters work against new forms of slavery.

Over the centuries, many other religious institutes received the Rule of Saint Augustine. In quite a few foundations, whether medieval or modern, this was the result of a decision in canon law aimed at limiting the number of religious rules. The depth of Augustine's spiritual inspiration proved to vary in those communities, and so some institutes ended up abandoning this patronage.

## The Face of Augustine

Thus many consecrated men and women turn to the rule and the spirituality of the shepherd of Hippo to inspire their everyday life. Through these communities, Augustine's voice continues to resound, offering his harmonious, demanding, and hope-filled teaching. Through them, his hand still stretches out to those who seek the truth and beauty. Through them, the face of Augustine still bends over the poor of every sort, offering the smiling mercy that was one of his treasures. Through them, there are oases open to the people of this time, in which the radical Gospel message of humility and poverty is made tangible; places where, despite human weakness, unity in charity makes itself joyously visible.

Abbeys, monasteries, and convents are open for meetings, spiritual accompaniment, or retreats, because they often have a guesthouse. The faithful or those seeking God can thus experience that Augustine is alive in the Church.

www.abbaye-stmaurice.ch
www.chanoines-du-latran.com
www.gsbernard.ch
www.mondaye.com
www.frigolet.com
www.abbaye-de-leffe.be
www.chanoines-saint-victor.fr
www.lagrasse.org
www.augustines-malestroit.com
www.soeursdazille.com
www.assomption.org